RAISING
GIANT-
KILLERS

RAISING GIANT-KILLERS

RELEASING YOUR CHILD'S DIVINE DESTINY
through INTENTIONAL PARENTING

BILL JOHNSON

WITH BENI JOHNSON

Chosen
a division of Baker Publishing Group
Minneapolis, Minnesota

© 2018 by BRevived, LLC

Published by Chosen Books
11400 Hampshire Avenue South
Bloomington, Minnesota 55438
www.chosenbooks.com

Chosen Books is a division of
Baker Publishing Group, Grand Rapids, Michigan

ISBN 978-0-8007-9923-6 (cloth)
ISBN 978-0-8007-9939-7 (ITPE)

Printed in the United States of America

Library of Congress Cataloging-in-Publication Data
Names: Johnson, Bill, author.
Title: Raising giant-killers : releasing your child's divine destiny through intentional parenting / Bill Johnson with Beni Johnson.
Description: Minneapolis : Chosen, a division of Baker Publishing Group, 2018.
Identifiers: LCCN 2018040724| ISBN 9780800799236 (cloth : alk. paper) | ISBN 9781493417360 (e-book)
Subjects: LCSH: Parenting—Religious aspects—Christianity. | Child rearing—Religious aspects—Christianity. | Individual differences in children. | Individual differences—Religious aspects—Christianity.
Classification: LCC BV4529 .J633 2018 | DDC 248.8/45—dc23
LC record available at https://lccn.loc.gov/2018040724

Cover design by LOOK Design Studio

19 20 21 22 23 24 25   8 7 6 5 4 3

We dedicate this book to our three children:

Eric, Brian and Leah.

You are a dream come true.
The privilege of being your parents is the greatest of all honors.
We love you beyond words, and are thankful for your role
as parents, leaders and world-changers.
We celebrate you wholeheartedly. And now we watch and pray
as you lovingly raise our ten grandchildren.
You are our ultimate joy in life.

Contents

Contents

Acknowledgments

Many thanks to my personal staff—Michael and Abigail. Your constant help is priceless to me, making books like this possible.

And many thanks to Pam Spinosi—your help with *Raising Giant-Killers* goes beyond words. Your editing skill and your advice in the process have once again proven to be of supreme value. Thanks!

Introduction

Parenting with Divine Purpose

W<small>E WROTE THIS BOOK</small> from our experience. We went into parenting with the dream that we could enjoy each season of our children's lives more than the previous one. We also felt we were not to be bound or influenced by the negativity found in the normal home. By the grace of God, we watched this dream become reality.

There are many wonderful books on parenting, written by extremely competent authors and leaders. We truly celebrate them all, as we need all the insight and training for this challenging task that we can possibly get. This book, however, is written not to duplicate their efforts or echo their insights. Instead, we hope to add to the message a sense of the privilege of raising children with an unwavering divine purpose. This is our passion—to *raise giant-killers* who will change the world. Together, we must alter the course of world history.

Bill and Beni Johnson

David, Goliath and You

THE IDEA OF RAISING OUR CHILDREN to be *giant-killers* may seem too violent a metaphor for some and too farfetched for others. But for me, it is an extremely accurate description of parenting, at least for those who want to raise their children with eternal significance.

The psalmist accurately described this challenge and privilege with these words: "Behold, children are a gift of the LORD . . . like arrows in the hand of a warrior . . ." (Psalm 127:3–4). This passage reveals the two primary parts of being a mom or dad—the joy of receiving the gift of a child from God, and the sobering responsibility of training the child for significance. The parent who values the gift will benefit most from its impact.

In biblical days bows, arrows, swords and spears were the primary tools for warfare. A warrior would much prefer dealing with an enemy at a distance with an arrow to doing hand-to-hand combat with a sword or spear. The point is, the bow and arrow were preferred instruments of war. The warrior had to have a sufficient number of arrows in his possession if he was going to engage the enemy with any measure of confidence. And those arrows had to be tried and true—fully capable of functioning according to their design.

This psalm gives us an unusual insight into the measure of confidence parents have in spiritual warfare when they have raised their children with eternal purpose. A child functioning according to his or her gift and design wreaks havoc on the powers of darkness. This is a side benefit to raising children correctly. Just as wise business leaders know how to make their money work for them even when they sleep, so it is with parenting. Our investment brings a return long after our children are out of our direct influence and focus. Raising children correctly brings spiritual dividends to our whole family line, even after the children are raised and out of the house.

In The Passion Translation, Psalm 127:5 reads this way:

> Happy will be the couple who has many of them! A household full of children will not bring shame on your name but victory when you face your enemies, for your offspring will have influence and honor to prevail on your behalf!

Perhaps a word of caution is needed at this point: Children are not tools to be used for personal gain. In a sense, they are not even ours. They are on loan from God, and it is our responsibility to steward correctly God's treasure in a way that pleases Him. Doing this right brings long-term benefits and influence on our family line for many generations.

Born into Conflict

We were born into a war. Every one of us. Even Adam and Eve were given the assignment to "subdue" the earth (Genesis 1:28), implying that there was disorder outside the Garden of Eden they lived in. They were given the responsibility to manage and expand the boundaries of that Garden until the whole earth mirrored its order and beauty.

Eden was the place of perfect peace and beauty. If the whole earth had become like the Garden, then God would have taken back a place of chaos through those made in His image, who functioned in relationship with Him. Living joyfully under God's influence, they were the ones who were to rule. As such, they carried His authority as His delegated ones.

Adam and Eve's sin disrupted the plan for peace and order that God had intended for the entire planet. Instead of subduing the earth, they were subdued by the one they obeyed—the serpent. Then Jesus, the eternal Son of God, became a man to accomplish on our behalf what we could not do for ourselves. As such, He is called the *last Adam*. The first Adam brought death into the world. The last Adam brought life:

> For if by the transgression of the one, death reigned through the one, much more those who receive the abundance of grace and of the gift of righteousness will reign in life through the One, Jesus Christ.
>
> Romans 5:17

He defeated sin, the grave and the powers of darkness on our behalf. This is the context into which all are born. We all were born into this war that has already been won. Because of this, we can be confident in our having been positioned for triumph. Jesus was victorious on our behalf, which makes our victory possible. And now, although still at war, we fight from victory. Not for it.

Take note of the phrase "reign in life through the One, Jesus Christ." Because of Jesus, parents and children alike are to reign in life. Reigning in life is not reigning over people. It is not about the power of title or position. Reigning in life means that money does not control me. I manage it for the glory of God. Conflict does not control me. I control my response to problems in a way that represents Jesus accurately. Reigning in life is part of the inheritance for all who follow Him. It is time to become completely absorbed in this mandate!

Our Struggle

The apostle Paul described the normal Christian life with these words:

> For our struggle is not against flesh and blood, but against the rulers, against the powers, against the world forces of this darkness, against the spiritual forces of wickedness in the heavenly places.
>
> Ephesians 6:12

Here Paul addresses the different realms of demonic influence. That we were born into a war should help us understand the *why* behind many of the conflicts and difficulties we face in life. The devil failed in stopping the redemptive work of Jesus and now tries to blemish the effect of that work in how we do life. The war is about our place with God the Father and our identity in Christ.

It is important to understand this spiritual reality of warring for our identity in Christ as the platform for parenting. This is the context into which our children are born. I know this may sound rather gruesome, but it is real. On the other hand, it is the victorious Christ who gives us reason to hope far above the intimidating threat of our present spiritual battles. And hope is what fuels the home of every family that lives under the influence of the Spirit of God.

The greatest news about true spiritual warfare is that it is not devil focused. I know that sounds strange, but it is true. It really is focused on Jesus, the Son of God. Our greatest victories come in the celebration of His goodness and presence. Glorifying God may not seem like warfare to many, but it is often warfare in the purest form. Anytime the focus of prayer or worship is fighting the devil, it is no longer prayer or worship.

The psalmist wrote, "Let God arise, let His enemies be scattered" (Psalm 68:1). God arises in praise, and the enemies are scattered as a result. And again, "Let the high praises of God be in their mouth, and a two-edged sword in their hand" (Psalm 149:6). Here victory unfolds as we celebrate and honor Him with praise. Our praise has an effect on our surroundings, as though we were wielding a two-edged sword. My wife deals with this combination of subjects brilliantly in her book *The Happy Intercessor*.*

A Shepherd Boy

The biblical story of David and Goliath has become so well-known in society that their names are often used to describe someone overcoming impossible odds in sports, business or politics. We have seen the mom-and-pop business go up against a big corporation and win a decisive victory in the courts, against all odds. Similar stories exist in the sporting world, as the great underdog defeats a team or individual who was far superior in everyone's estimation. We have also witnessed the unheard-of politician who seems to come out of nowhere to defeat an incumbent or a highly favored opponent. This happens much to the surprise of the media and political experts. And in all these stories, the headlines read something to this effect: "David Beats Goliath Again."

While these are accurate uses of the story in measure, the actual record of the David and Goliath conflict is so much greater. First of all, I remind you, David was a young shepherd boy who stood up in spite of Israel's history of fearing giants.

There is no reason to believe that David was raised to be a world-changer. His father basically forgot him when the prophet Samuel came to pick a son of Jesse to be king. Every other son seemed a more logical choice than his youngest. They were bigger, brighter and more favored by their dad. It is quite possible that David was an illegitimate child of Jesse. That would explain the ill treatment from his father and brothers. But what is illegitimate to some is often prized and chosen by God. A child born out of wedlock is a physical reminder that only in God's economy can life come out of sin. As the Great Redeemer, God is good at treasuring what people

*See Beni Johnson, *The Happy Intercessor* (Destiny Image, 2009).

reject. Regardless of his beginnings, David grew up against the odds and became significant through the sovereign touch of God on his life.

When David went up against Goliath, he was confronting Israel's own history. The fear of giants is what kept them from the Promised Land in the first place. And now a young man shows nothing but contempt for this giant who taunts the armies of the living God. This attitude is something you cannot fake. David felt disgust for this one who was now blaspheming the name of the Lord. When you walk with God as David did, feeling jealous for His name is normal and healthy.

How It All Started

The first generation of Israelites stayed out of the Promised Land because they feared the giants. Twelve spies went into the land to see what they were about to inherit. Ten of them came out very fearful, thinking they were sure to die if they went into battle against the inhabitants. Fear of giants kept the people of God away from what He had promised them. The ten spies actually gave this report:

> But the men who had gone up with him said, "*We are not able to go up* against the people, for they are too strong for us." So they gave out to the sons of Israel a bad report of the land which they had spied out, saying, "The land through which we have gone, in spying it out, is a land that devours its inhabitants; and *all the people whom we saw in it are men of great size*. There also we saw the Nephilim (the sons of Anak are part of the Nephilim); and *we became like grasshoppers in our own sight*, and so we were in their sight."
>
> Numbers 13:31–33, emphasis added

Their last statement is revealing: "We became like grasshoppers in our own sight." That is quite an insight about the people who were given an extraordinary promise from God. They saw the size of their enemy, and they saw the limitations of their size and training. What is tragic is that they lost sight of the size of their God and the size of their promise from God. This happens whenever we make the promises into being about ourselves, instead of being about God fulfilling His purposes in the earth. He answers our prayers and fulfills His promises for the sake of His name.

The vision both the Israelites and those ten spies had because of the promise was replaced by a view of the giants. Seeing any part of our lives, whether our past, present or future, without God at the center is seeing a lie. Yet two of the twelve spies were excited to have the opportunity of conquering the ones the others feared. Forty years later, it came time for Israel to try again to obtain the promise of God. Interestingly, when it came time for the land to be divided according to tribes and families, Caleb, one of the two faithful original spies, asked Joshua for the hill country where the giants lived. The *capital city of their fears* was to be his inheritance. He asked for the privilege of defeating them! I love this part of the story so much. He had to wait forty years to obtain his promise, because of the fear caused by the bad report the ten spies had given. Unbelief and fear are both contagious. But he did not catch that disease. He preserved and built his faith, until it was time to receive his own inheritance. Caleb asked for the stronghold of the giants for his home. Brilliant!

I realize that this is not directly about parenting, but in a sense, it is. This is forming a Kingdom attitude. It is about a lifestyle of courage that honors God. Stirring up and living with a courageous attitude is what parents and grandparents must do. We have to learn to draw from every biblical example we can find. We must also refuse to be impressed by the size of the giants we face. They are not worthy of the attention. God has already gone before us and set the stage for our triumph through the promises He has given us.

If your answer to prayer is delayed, it is gaining interest. And when breakthrough comes, it will come with greater power and glory than if it had been released at the moment you first prayed. Live with that confidence in all of life. But be certain of doing this with the wonderful privilege of raising *giant-killers*. God designed our children to carry courage into all the earth. They were born for this.

How do you view your ability to raise children? Are you more aware of your inability than you are of God's ability to help you? Are you more aware of the evil that pervades society than you are of the righteousness of God in your own life? Do you have the "I'm a grasshopper compared to the giant I face" perspective? If so, repent. Confess and forsake the lie. God is present. And He has a promise tailor-made for you. The opportunity for significance is before you. Don't allow your giant to kill the momentum of faith that God has designed for your entire family line. Embrace David and Caleb's attitude of assured victory. And remember this important lesson: Self-confidence is no greater than self. God confidence, which is called *faith*, is as big as God.

A Forty-Year-Old Promise

The next generation of Israelites overcame the fear of their enemies, giving God a chance to demonstrate that He was the author of the promise. One of the most vital Kingdom principles for us is that *God enables what He promises.* Israel inherited what God had said they would inherit, although it was forty years after God had originally intended. Rebellion on our end changes God's timing.

Israel had made a lot of progress in regard to giants and walking in their Promised Land. After they went into the land to receive their inheritance, we never hear of the giants again until now, with their army facing Goliath. There is something to be said about having to reaffirm our confidence in God by facing our own giants. If a giant remains in our land, it is so we can discover what God has given us. The enemy always tries to make us more aware of our problems than of the solutions we carry.

David was not just facing a giant. He was facing what Israel had feared from their days in the wilderness, and he was displaying courage about their past, present and future. He was confronting their past by pursuing the nemesis to their identity as God's people. He was challenging their present by bringing revenge upon the one who would mock the name of the living God. And he was defying Goliath's attempt to bring Israel back into slavery, ensuring a more secure and successful future. This was a young shepherd boy facing this challenge. We raise our children knowing that as God empowers them, they are powerful. Even in their youth. We teach them their identity and purpose, with their destiny in mind.

David picked up five stones, although one would be all he needed for Goliath. Unbelief did not cause him to pick up too many. David obviously was overflowing with faith and great confidence. Goliath had brothers. It is generally thought that David was prepared to finish the task at hand, should the other four attack him. In raising children of significance, it is important to raise them with the commitment to finish the task.

The destiny of nations hung in the balance as a young shepherd boy went up against the giant the armies of Israel feared. As one friend told us so many years ago, children do not receive a junior Holy Ghost! He only comes in one size—omnipresent and all-powerful.

The Source of Extraordinary Courage

David had a heart for God that permeated everything he did. He was known as a worshiper. But that lifestyle started long before he became king. He learned how God loved to respond to him as he offered up the sacrifice of thanksgiving and praise. This was on the backside of the desert, while leading his father's sheep. He became courageous because God responded to him. It was not because he was raised that way.

While I believe that as parents we make a large contribution to our child's level of courage, the bottom line is that our greatest contribution is to introduce our children to a heavenly Father who is moved by their hearts' cry. They must see for themselves that He responds to their offerings of thanksgiving and praise. We can move God! Nothing is greater than seeing that the God of the universe is moved by our prayers. That is the source of extraordinary courage. And our challenge to build that into our children requires an example, instruction and the opportunity.

David reaffirmed the past, brought peace to the present and secured a more confident future. Because you have the courage to raise your child to make a difference, your child will have the fuel he or she needs to become the courageous one. Model this courageous lifestyle as best you know how.

Giant-Killers, Unite!

I am not sure who said it first, but my dear friend James Goll has often said, "If God allows a Goliath in front of you, then He knows there is a David inside of you."

The David and Goliath story is the one story about defeating giants that is common knowledge both in and out of the Church. Yet there were several giants killed in the Bible, and followers of David killed them all.

If we want our children to become giant-killers, we must face and destroy our own giants. Our example and momentum will become their inheritance.

2

Raising Parents

ANNING LIEBSCHER, leader and founder of the amazing Jesus Culture ministry that has now become a movement, tells a hilarious story about taking his dog in for training. This dog was a nuisance and a constant frustration for Banning's entire family. But they loved the dog and wanted it to remain part of their household. Banning hoped that a professional dog trainer could fix its apparent issues. He found a reputable trainer and paid in advance for an entire eight-week class to attend with other dogs and owners. But Banning quit after two weeks. The instructor never once worked with the dog one-on-one. At least 95 percent of the time, she tried to work only with Banning.

If I have a dog that does not pay attention to me, repeatedly disobeys me and breaks the commonsense rules of my house, I want the trainer to fix the problem. Obviously, the problem is the dog! Yet this trainer concluded that Banning was the real problem. Banning did not take his dog to the trainer to have the trainer preach at him. He paid good money so his dog could be cured of its issues. Looking back at my history with my own dog, a somewhat crazy German shorthaired pointer, I am pretty certain I was the problem, too. Banning and I are probably the people the dog trainers talk about when they get together for coffee.

The subject of raising children really does start with the nature, character and condition of the parents. It does not take perfect parents to raise children correctly. Nor do the parents have to come from healthy backgrounds. But it does take the intentional pursuit of the values rooted in what the Bible calls the *Kingdom of God*. And quite honestly, many who have never even heard of the Kingdom have succeeded at this task through the years. The principles of that Kingdom are profoundly written in the hearts of people so that all can obey them.

It may surprise you, but those who steward these principles, even if they are not born again, have a profound effect on the children they raise. I have seen unbelievers model the truths of the Kingdom with great results. And I have seen believers ignore those principles with devastating results in the lives of their children. Truth is truth, and it benefits anyone who puts value on it through obedience and respect. It should be noted, however, that anyone who has a personal relationship with Jesus and lives by the principles of His world would always have the advantage over anyone who simply values heavenly concepts.

Perfectly Imperfect

There are not a lot of people who were raised by Kingdom-oriented parents. By *Kingdom-oriented*, I mean parents who raised their children with the values of God's world and who worked to build something in their children that only faith could envision. Most parents simply did their best, which is something to be thankful for. But even some of the best parents gave little consideration to the idea that they could raise their children to have eternal impact. Since God is the one who makes it possible to live without impossibility, I figure we might as well live beyond what is acceptable and normal.

There have also been parents who were evil to the core. Through abuse and neglect, these parents declared to their children that having kids just got in the way of their self-centered plans for their lives. Some of the most remarkable testimonies of all are of children who were raised in that hellish environment, only to become champions of godliness who have eternal purpose. They in turn go on to raise their children in the ways of the Lord as the ultimate vindication for what they did not have. I honor these heroes of the faith with everything in me. Their story is the essence of beauty and redemption.

Regardless of our background, a perfect, generous, kind and loving Father is now raising us. We all, whether with wonderful or horrible upbringings, are responsible to have our history recalibrated by walking with a Father who is perfect in every way. And while there are many who naturally project the failures and weaknesses of their earthly parents onto their heavenly Father, don't use that kind of reasoning as an excuse. Learn what God is like, and let that become a cornerstone of thought from this point on. It is only by grace that any one of us can represent Him well.

Even though I had a godly mom and dad, having children of my own was the time when I started learning about my heavenly Father in a way that I never knew was possible. I felt things for my children that I had never felt before. Having righteousness prevail in my early years certainly gave me a head start. Yet seeing my own heart explode with love and affection for these three dear ones whom God entrusted into my care ushered in a whole new day.

My Parents

The godly parents who raised me had a vision of me accomplishing much with my life. Yet they never tried to force or coerce me into a specific direction. They were a constant source of encouragement, telling me that I could achieve anything I set my mind on. They championed me in my interests and pursuits.

Parents who are authentic, humble and truly hungry for whatever God has in store for their lives are positioned to raise real world-changers. It is the sense of adventure and mystery that becomes the contagious ingredient. Embracing our life's assignment as a mysterious journey is a great start to a lifetime of surprises and personal fulfillment.

Survival is a pitiful goal for parenting. We have been given heaven's treasure, with the assignment to build something of eternal significance. As we examined in the David and Goliath story, courage is an essential ingredient for life—especially when it comes to building a home.

The Purpose of Parenting

There is a passage in Malachi that has spoken strongly to me for many years on the reasons for becoming godly parents. In fact, God gets much more specific. Scripture teaches that in marriage, two people become one. Marriage is a mystery between a husband and wife that points prophetically to Jesus and His Bride, the Church. And yet, as it pertains to the natural family, God had the idea of two becoming one for a reason. The passage addresses it clearly, and while reading it in several translations helps clarify this issue, the New Living Translation speaks the most clearly to me:

> Didn't the LORD make you one with your wife? In body and spirit you are his. And what does he want? Godly children from your union. So guard your heart; remain loyal to the wife of your youth. "For I hate divorce!" says the LORD, the God of Israel. "To divorce your wife is to overwhelm her with cruelty," says the LORD of Heaven's Armies. "So guard your heart; do not be unfaithful to your wife." *or* husband
>
> Malachi 2:15–16

God is not shy about His intentions. He created the miracle of two people becoming one. But His reason for this spiritual event is that He desires godly offspring to come forth from that union. Consider the implications of this statement. Unity is the context in

"Raising children to live with purpose in a light matter and make a difference

which children become their best, with the greatest chance of stepping into eternal significance. This is not to say that children cannot grow up with a heart for God even in a divided home. Evidence is everywhere that God's grace is more than sufficient to make up for what is lacking in every household. Yet His purpose remains intact. When two become one, it sets the stage for godly children to be raised and empowered to go into the world and have a godly impact.

God desires that His nature be seen in the earth. He longs for all of creation to benefit from the manifestation of His heart through His delegated ones, people. Understanding this truth helps us fulfill our call as representatives of God our Father in the earth.

God Revealed

God's nature is most clearly revealed through the redemptive story of Jesus and His suffering on the cross on our behalf. There is no greater story, nor is there a stronger message. It is vital that we illustrate this reality through carrying our own cross, entering into the resurrection life. Both integrity and power become the manifestations of our redeemed lives.

The Father restores us to our purpose and design in our salvation. This becomes visible through the characteristics of integrity and power. But those things are to be the manifestations of being in perfect harmony with Him, revealing Him in all we do and are. His redeemed ones must rediscover and enjoy that sense of purpose.

God is gloriously revealed in the Gospel. But He is also made known through His creation, through art, people and design. The list is endless. But one of the clearest ways He is to be revealed is in the home—in how we live as husband, wife and children. When God says that His purpose in marriage is godly offspring, He is looking for a generation who would grow up in our homes to model and reflect His nature in all they say and do. This is to become a generation of those who demonstrate His perfect rule over all He has made, modeling "on earth as it is in heaven."

*Sanctify —
free of sin,
purity*

Marriage Prophesies

Paul talked of marriage in the most sobering terms. He illustrated both the design and the sanctity of the home through Jesus' relationship with His Church, which, of course, refers to born-again people, not institutions or buildings:

> Husbands, love your wives, just as Christ also loved the church and gave Himself up for her, so that He might sanctify her, having cleansed her by the washing of water with the word, that He might present to Himself the church in all her glory, having no spot or wrinkle or any such thing; but that she would be holy and blameless. So husbands ought also to love their own wives as their own bodies. He who loves his own wife loves himself; for no one ever hated his own flesh, but nourishes and cherishes it, just as Christ also does the church, because we are members of His body.
>
> Ephesians 5:25–30

Parents who succeed here will find it much easier to raise children who are in touch with their own design and purpose to change the world. Once children have tasted the ongoing life in a family setting, they have basically been ruined for anything less. Even if they wander, they will remember and return to the place where there is life. We are all attracted to life.

Paul intentionally makes a profound comparison between Christ and the Church, and the husband and wife. The latter two illustrate in the natural the reality that exists in the spiritual. In fact, the natural becomes spiritual, in that the home becomes the place of the ultimate revelation of God's love for His Bride through the relationship of a husband and wife.

Please notice a few things from the Ephesians 5 passage. Jesus "gave Himself up" completely for the Church. This standard creates the atmosphere of purpose and design that children were intended to grow up in. Their childhood then becomes a time of exposure to heavenly values that become a blueprint for relationships. If you can succeed here, you can succeed anywhere.

Also notice that His word over her brings cleansing and refreshing. This is quite different from many relationships in which the home is where people become more loose with conversation instead of more careful. My words to my wife are to refresh, encourage and help bring her into her destiny. The one who loves his wife well *loves himself well*. Perhaps weakness in the area of *self-love* is one of the causes of weak family life, for the one who is weak in his love for himself has not received well the abundant love of God. We love well because we have received love well. We can only give away what we have received.

The Ideal and the Reality

As parents, we are builders of families, individuals and legacies. It is vital to live with an idea of what we are building, that we might be more intentional. With that is an inherent awareness of the price we must pay to obtain such a great reward.

The most ideal building blocks are a husband and wife in love, in unity. That context is hard to beat. And yet I know many single parents who have done remarkable jobs raising their children. The combination of God's grace and their dedication to make up for what was missing launched them into a realm of success that many couples never enter. It must be noted that *two are better than one, if united. But two are less than one, if divided.*

Some parents are single through tragedy. Some are single through sins committed against them. And then there are those who find themselves alone because of their own wrong choices. Regardless of how it happened, please know that God forgives and heals. He alone can make one equal two in effectiveness and outcome. He alone gives that sort of grace.

We must also recognize that any parent who is raising his or her children to be world-changers, giant-killers, is doing so by the grace of God. His enablement makes the impossible possible. He deserves all the glory.

Following Sheep

Several times, Scripture says that the shepherd boy David followed his father's sheep. Shepherds are known for leading sheep to water, food and safety. Yet special notice was given to David's unusual method of leadership:

> Now therefore, thus you shall say to My servant David, "Thus says the LORD of hosts, 'I took you from the pasture, *from following the sheep*, to be ruler over My people Israel.'"
>
> 2 Samuel 7:8, emphasis added

Not only was David's way of leadership given special mention; it was identified as the platform from which he was launched into his role as king. *From following . . . to be ruler.*

All parenting principles are leadership principles, God's way. As parents, we lead. There is no question that leadership requires that we go places and people follow. But there is a role in leadership that is seldom talked about—the humility that is also willing to follow.

All good leaders know they don't know everything. That is a great beginning place for developing humility. Having the awareness of personal need creates a hunger that takes us from comfort and complacency to sacrifice and learning. But knowledge turns to wisdom when we know where we go to learn. Often it can be said that the learning we need the most is where we would least likely go on our own, without God's instruction to do so.

Learning from Children

We pay attention to those we lead, and at times we follow them. We hear, feel and value their perspective on things. But Jesus took this concept to a whole new level, as He intensified significantly the instruction for us to operate in humility. He exalted the role of children in the eyes of all who follow Him:

> And He called a child to Himself and set him before them, and said, "Truly I say to you, unless you are converted and *become like children*, you will not enter the kingdom of heaven. Whoever then humbles himself *as this child, he is the greatest* in the kingdom of heaven. And whoever *receives one such child* in My name *receives Me*; but whoever causes one of these little ones who believe in Me to stumble, it would be better for him to have a heavy millstone hung around his neck, and to be drowned in the depth of the sea."
>
> Matthew 18:2–6, emphasis added

> But when Jesus saw this, He was indignant and said to them, "*Permit the children to come* to Me; do not hinder them; for the kingdom of God belongs to such as these. Truly I say to you, whoever *does not receive* the kingdom of God *like a child will not enter* it at all."
>
> Mark 10:14–15, emphasis added

Jesus taught His disciples that they had to *become like a child*. Their ability to lead was connected to their ability to follow. And while they were obviously followers of Jesus, He directed their attention to follow the lead of children. This is not in conflict with our need for maturity. It is just that sometimes what we consider to be maturity hardens us to the reality of the Kingdom, and practically speaking, is just plain boring. Life is such an adventure that boredom should never be the description of our lives. Anyone who is bored might want to examine how closely he or she is following Jesus, as He is anything but unexciting.

Parents who are unwilling to learn from their children are missing their greatest opportunity for growth. Pride and arrogance often work to keep us from our God moments in disguise. Parents with pride and arrogance issues are usually the most likely to create an

31

Need to stop being prideful and arrogant

atmosphere where they are the boss and in charge, but no one is following joyfully.

Time to Grow Down

definitely true

Children love adventure, easily forgive, are resilient, have an insatiable appetite for learning, value simple things, laugh throughout the day, imitate others without inhibition and are humble. These traits bring them into the highest place of honor, as Jesus says they are the greatest in His Kingdom. This really is astonishing. God's Kingdom is filled with extremes in beauty, wonder, excellence and heroes. And yet the greatest in that lineup are children. The beautiful thing is that everyone has access to this kind of greatness. It is greatness of the heart. Everyone has some measure of the desire for significance. It is not based on mere human talent or even God-given gifts. It is seen in the childlike person who still enjoys life. We must fight against anything and everything that works to steal our childlikeness in loving and serving God. This is one mountain worth fighting for.

Jesus also taught us the importance of receiving children, which is to accept, value and celebrate them. There are two fruits or benefits to receiving a child that are worth noting. First of all, in the Matthew 18 passage, if we receive a child, we receive Jesus. So many of our songs and sermons frequently mention our need for more of the presence of God in our lives. Perhaps *the more of Him* we long for is found in the measure in which we receive children. Taking time for children is receiving Him. He takes it personally, and He becomes manifest for us through the life of that child we receive.

The second time He mentions receiving children, in the Mark 10 passage, He connects it to our entrance into the Kingdom. Since the Kingdom is the realm of His dominion, it stands to reason that in the measure in which we receive children, in that measure we enter His rule, tasting of the benefit of His Kingdom. This really is astonishing, as our heart's cry is for His world. We enter it through this unusual door called "welcoming and celebrating children into our lives."

When My *No* Came Out Wrong

We once rented out a well-known Christian retreat center with cabins, a dining hall and large meeting rooms for our family reunion. It was a bit surreal to see over 160 people fly in from all over the world to attend. Some of them were missionaries who came from faraway lands just to reconnect with family members they had not seen for years, or with those they had never met.

We met together to worship, pray and have fun. Besides the recreational activities, there were breakout sessions with different subjects and themes. We even had panel discussions to address specific topics pertinent to our influence on the world environment we live in. To say this was a different kind of family reunion is a great understatement.

I remember at one point, the reunion coordinator announced to us all that something like 65 of the attendees were pastors or missionaries, or were their direct descendants. There were also a number of lawyers, university professors and people of various professional occupations. It was awe inspiring, and a bit intimidating as well. It is wonderful to be able to say that some of the most honoring people in the group were those of the *highest status* according to human accomplishment. They were the servants of all, with the most tender hearts, ready to celebrate the slightest victory others in the group shared. They still burned with a genuine love for Jesus. Amazing!

There was even a square dance, as some of my relatives were really into that. Not me, though. I don't dance for anyone. (Except for Jesus. I will dance before Him.) There is not anyone who can talk me out of such things once my mind is made up. And my mind had been made up on that subject for decades. That is a fact my whole family will attest to. Peer pressure means nothing to me. I attended, just to be social. As I stood there watching a room full of people laughing and tripping over their own feet, I enjoyed their pleasure. I also felt quite secure in my resolve not to dance.

Out of nowhere my daughter, Leah, who was eight at the time, came up to me and asked, "Daddy, will you dance with me?"

I could not believe what came out of my mouth. Somehow, my *No* came out wrong: "Sure, honey, I'll dance with you."

Every bit of stubborn resolve was dismantled in a moment by an eight-year-old. I had no protection against such a tactic. It was painful and embarrassing, until I saw her joy. I "received" the child and entered her joy, and I had such a wonderful time bringing delight to a little girl who means the world to me. In a way, this is what parenting looks like.

Welcoming a Visitation of God

As we think about these statements Jesus made about children, the Kingdom and His presence, it makes sense that the greatest place of visitation and breakthrough should be the family. It is the "two or three gathered in His name," permanently, that attracts His glorious presence (see Matthew 18:20). As parents and grandparents, we are positioned to receive the ultimate treasure, called *His Kingdom*, by receiving His ultimate treasure, called *children*. They come together in one package.

As parents, we must develop and protect our learning heart, always becoming more and more like children. Building home life around these kinds of values and lifestyles makes it easier to see how children can thrive until they become all God intended them to be.

The final point in Jesus' instructions on valuing children concerns what happens to those who cause children to stumble. This must be one of the more sobering statements about parenting in the Bible. We are stewards of a child's life. He or she does not belong to us, but is on loan. How we care for a child reveals how well we understand this concept of stewardship.

Many tithe, give offerings and invest money wisely, all because they know they are stewards of God's money. But tragically, these same people will often neglect or abuse a child out of personal frustration or selfishness, not realizing that the greatest earthly treasure they will ever be given is the life of that child. And we will have to give an account of what we did with that privileged assignment. To cause children to stumble is to cause them to make mistakes. Paul addresses this in Ephesians 6:4, when he states, "Fathers, do not provoke your children to anger." To *provoke* means "to stimulate one to a negative emotional reaction." Unhealthy parenting often provokes children to anger. Becoming healthy on the inside is the greatest thing I can do for my children.

The home can be a place where in carelessness parents provoke and intimidate children to undesirable reactions. It would be incorrect to assume that all negative reactions are the fault of the parent. But sometimes they are. And they often happen because of the parent's need to feel powerful before his or her child. These things ought not to be.

Following sheep, learning from our children and staying in the adventure throughout adulthood would certainly help in this privileged assignment of being a parent. Children learn as they go through life. Perhaps that is one of the traits required of being a good parent—the humility and willingness to learn as we go.

- Learn from our children, help them through the process by not being prideful and arrogant just to feel powerful in front of them.

- Remember they are loan to you. they will learn us they go.

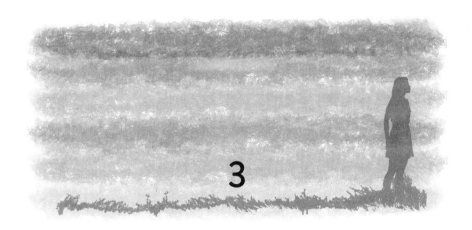

3

Parents as Teachers

WHEN I BECAME A PASTOR, I took my responsibilities for ministering the Word of God very seriously. I spent much time in prayer and in the Word. I was quick to discover that it was best if I did not study so that I would have a message to preach. It was so much healthier for me to study so I could learn. Period. And from my personal experience, I would try to teach the Scriptures. That approach changed everything.

I was a husband, a dad and a pastor, so it can be said that my two main concerns were family and the church. I did not want to succeed at pastoring a church, but fail in leading my family, so family became a primary focus in my study of Scripture. I looked for every chapter, verse or even phrase that would help me be a better husband and father. To be completely honest, I did not need as much study for being a good husband. That came somewhat naturally, since I had grown up with such great examples of being a good husband (in my father and grandfathers). And while it could be said that parenting was easy in measure for the same reason, I surely needed even more insight for being a good dad. I wanted so much more from my role as a father. To put it plainly, I wanted to raise giant-killers! Pure and simple. I wanted to raise children who would influence the course of world history. My Bible quickly became marked up with underlines and circles around the verses that gave me insight for this privileged assignment.

One of the first things I began to learn as a young parent was that God had given Beni and me the responsibility to teach and train our children. The more I searched the Word of God, the more I became convinced that it was my job, not that of the Church or government. These other institutions are gifted to supplement what happens in the home.

Biblical Culture

I love reading and studying the book of Deuteronomy. In my opinion, it is the book that shaped the culture of Israel more than any other. Culture is that system of beliefs, relational boundaries and values that creates a context in which a family, city or country thrives. In this case, we are talking about Israel, the people of God. Israel is also the precursor to the Church. Both Israel and the Church live and die by the culture they choose to live in.

In Deuteronomy, we find one thing made very clear: Parents have the responsibility to teach their children. There is little question that others are also involved in this privilege, but the primary ones responsible are the parents:

> Only give heed to yourself and keep your soul diligently, so that you *do not forget the things which your eyes have seen* and they do not depart from your heart all the days of your life; but *make them known to your sons and your grandsons*. Remember the day you stood before the LORD your God at Horeb, when the LORD said to me, "Assemble the people to Me, that I may *let them hear My words* so they may learn to fear Me all the days they live on the earth, and *that they may teach their children*."
>
> Deuteronomy 4:9–10, emphasis added

38

First of all, notice that they were to remember what they had seen. This was the group of people who had been brought out of Egypt with miracles, signs and wonders. Their life was one astonishing experience after another, interspersed with enemies and challenges to their faith. Remembering God's activities among them would be critical to their victory, as He is more than a philosophy or concept. He is God, the ever-present God.

Israel was also required to stand and listen to the Word of God. Hearing what God requires and expects of people would cause them to fear Him. This is the kind of fear that does not drive people away from God, but instead, endears Him to them. And if they listened and obtained a fear of God, they would be positioned to teach the same to their children. Frequently throughout Scripture, we see God making it possible for something to be obtained by one generation and also imparted to the next so there is never a decline in the intent and purpose of the people of God on earth. He only goes from glory to glory and has positioned us to do the same.

Notice the context for teaching our children that this next passage reveals:

> *You shall teach them diligently to your sons* and shall talk of them when you sit in your house and when you walk by the way and when you lie down and when you rise up. You shall bind them as a sign on your hand and they shall be as frontals on your forehead. You shall write them on the doorposts of your house and on your gates.
>
> Deuteronomy 6:7–9, emphasis added

You teach your children *when you sit, walk, lie down and rise up.* In other words, the time to teach is when you are experiencing life together. Instead of only creating a slot of teaching time, make life itself a lesson. A word of warning—preachy-type instruction gets old fast. But when we embrace the adventure called life and we discover it together, every occasion is the perfect occasion for learning insight and skills.

At our Easter Sunrise Service, we had breakfast for our members at different homes in our church. Brian was around four years old at the time, and he was only interested in eating a cinnamon roll. I wanted him to eat his eggs first. He refused. I remembered that Jesus endured the cross "for the joy set before Him" (Hebrews 12:2). So I held the roll in front of him, to motivate him to eat his eggs. He stared at it, and he finally finished the eggs. I rewarded him with the wonderful roll. This is life in the Kingdom. It all matters.

It is so liberating to realize that life itself is the classroom, and that every day is school. Living conscious of opportunities and purpose makes the journey a shared one that parents and children get to enjoy. That means we have the privileged responsibility to live intentionally. No matter the circumstances, we do life with our children in mind.

I remember coming home from the office one day and finding Beni at the door, telling me I needed to come and see what Eric had done. She took me into the spare bedroom. Eric, who was then about five years old, had drawn all over one of the walls with crayons. Apparently, Beni had told him that she would have to tell me about it when I came home. He looked at me as if he were in trouble. He had filled about a ten-foot section of the wall with a drawing of a cityscape, including many structures and high-rise buildings. He even put windows in the buildings.

I was impressed. I looked at the wall and then looked at him and said, "You did a good job, son. I'm really impressed at the way you drew these buildings. Look at those windows. Great job." I then told him that the next time he wanted to draw, he should ask for paper. It would be a lot better that way, as it would not be so hard to clean.

It was kind of funny that within a week or so, we had guests over for dinner. During the meal, I interrupted our time together and said, "I need to show you something. Come and see." Then I showed them what Eric had done. This time Eric was there, with his head held high as I pointed to the details of his artwork. I don't

40

know if our friends were impressed, but it was not for them. It was for my son.

When we stay away from "preaching at our children," they are more likely to ask questions about life itself.

> *When your son asks* you in time to come, saying, "*What do the testimonies and the statutes and the judgments mean* which the LORD our God commanded you?" *then you shall say to your son,* "We were slaves to Pharaoh in Egypt, and the LORD brought us from Egypt with a mighty hand. Moreover, the LORD showed great and distressing signs and wonders before our eyes against Egypt, Pharaoh and all his household; He brought us out from there in order to bring us in, to give us the land which He had sworn to our fathers."
>
> Deuteronomy 6:20–23, emphasis added

Dialogue

Our children would much rather have dialogues with us than have to listen to monologues. Dialogue is two-way conversation that includes give-and-take, as well as sometimes learning together.

It is interesting that Israel was able to create a culture where children became curious about God and naturally had questions about the wonders He had done, the statutes or rules He had given them to abide by, and the judgments He had made. God was their Lord and King, and He was by choice a premiere part of their conversation.

Principles were to be taught and stories were to be told in the context of family life:

> For He established a testimony in Jacob and appointed a law in Israel, which He commanded our fathers that they should *teach them to their children*, that the generation to come might know, even the children yet to be born, that they may arise and *tell them to their children, that they should put their confidence in God* and not forget the works of God, but keep His commandments, and not be like their fathers, a stubborn and rebellious generation, a generation that did not prepare its heart and whose spirit was not faithful to God.
>
> Psalm 78:5–8, emphasis added

We must share our personal God-story so that our family members have a working knowledge of the nature and heart of God for us all. It was this process that set the stage for children to have a natural confidence in God. This is astonishing! If this process is done well, children instinctively trust God over everything else in life and have a natural resistance to the stubbornness of heart that so many in previous generations have been known for. This is the outcome for all of us who follow Jesus' desire. There is no greater joy in life: "I have no greater joy than this, to hear of my children walking in the truth" (3 John 4). This passage, of course, concerns spiritual children. How much more joy there is for us when these children are both our natural and spiritual children!

Testimonies Prophesy

Sharing testimonies is vital in building an awareness of the *God who is with us*, and the *God who is for us*. Any family that makes this a primary focus will experience great dividends. By nature, these stories carry the revelation of God's heart and nature, which never changes. That means when we hear a story of what God has done for someone else, we are hearing a story of what He would do for us. Remember, He is no respecter of persons, and He is the same yesterday, today and forever (see Acts 10:34; Romans 2:11; Hebrews 13:8). The great British preacher Charles Spurgeon spoke on this subject in his message "The Story of God's Mighty Acts" (emphasis added):

> When people hear about what God used to do, one of the things they say is, "Oh, that was a very long while ago." . . . I thought it was God that did it. Has God changed? Is he not an immutable God, the same yesterday, today and forever? Does that not furnish an argument to prove that what God has done at one time he can do at another? Nay, I think I may push it a little further, and say *what he has done once, is a prophecy of what he intends to do again*. . . . Whatever God has done . . . is to be looked upon as a precedent. . . . [Let us]

with earnestness seek that God would restore to us the faith of the men of old, that we may richly enjoy his grace as in the days of old.*

He got it right! This is the focus of Scripture, and it is the reason Israel was commanded to keep the testimony. Testimonies were the stories that were to become the lenses through which they could see their present challenge.

Our God is the God of the impossible, and He has made us to be a people of the impossible. Testimonies play a role in getting us ready for our life assignments of *killing giants* and shaping the course of world history.

Testimonies are fundamental building blocks of the awareness of God who is with us. They impart a conviction concerning His nature that must be displayed in and through us to the world. It is so common for problems, stories of tragedies and even gossip about other people's issues or failures to be shared at our dinner tables. What if we become more intentional in giving a testimony of something only God can do and get credit for? It changes everything for us—what we think about God, about ourselves and about our purpose in life.

Be sure to include for your children stories of friends and/or leaders who have credibility. These stories will become great treasures of the heart. Beni and I recently brought our three eldest grandchildren over to the house to share in a nice meal. I had had it in my heart for quite some time to share with them the details of my walk with God. We gave each of them a $50 bill, as a prophetic symbol of the Year of Jubilee. Jubilee was a very special event that happened in Israel every fifty years. During this year, all debts were forgiven and slaves were set free, as were prisoners. Jesus used the concept to illustrate what every year is like for the believer, calling it the "favorable year of the Lord." I asked my grandchildren not to spend their bill for

*Charles H. Spurgeon, "The Story of God's Might Acts," delivered at the Music Hall, Royal Surrey Gardens, found in *The New Park Street Pulpit Containing Sermons Preached and Revised by the Rev. C. H. Spurgeon, Minister of the Chapel, During the Year 1859: Volume V* (London, England: Passmore, Allabaster, & Sons, 1894), 309–10.

at least one year. I wanted for them to keep it visible, that it might remind them of the freedom that only Jesus can bring.

The stories I shared with them are ones they may not hear in a message, yet my descendants should know them. I told them of the moment I surrendered everything to Jesus, describing my hunger for Him as best I could. It was very important to me that they understood the price I paid to know Him more. It was not gruesome, but it was honest and challenging. I also described the most important encounters I have ever had with the Lord and what happened to me as a result. Then I laid my hands on them and prayed for God to mark them for His purposes, and I released great blessing over them. This is a direction I plan to follow with all my grandchildren.

Rewards

I also challenged my grandchildren to read my book *Defining Moments: God-Encounters with Ordinary People Who Changed the World* (Whitaker House, 2016). It contains the stories of thirteen people in Church history who were normal, everyday people who had unusual encounters with God—thus the name, *Defining Moments.* After their encounter, they became world-changers. Once a grandchild finishes the book, we meet together for around ninety minutes to discuss what he or she has read. I don't give a pass-or-fail quiz; it is a dialogue. We discuss each person, and then in greater detail the person who stands out to that child the most and why. After the evening is over, I pay my grandchild $500 for reading the book.

I don't want to suggest that we always need to pay our children to do things, or that you as a parent or grandparent should follow my example. What I do now would have been completely unreasonable for me as a parent thirty years ago. Things were very tight for us financially back then. It is also obvious that not everyone who wants to follow my lead will pay the same amount of money. I chose an amount that best represented my heart and my wallet. You can do the same. I just wanted you to know what I do now that I am able, and how I approach representing our heavenly Father, who is "a rewarder of those who seek Him" (Hebrews 11:6, emphasis added).

Rewards are an essential part of our lives, and it is up to us as parents to give them. But it would not be right or healthy to suggest that all rewards be money or food. These things can serve as a reward, but they mean little if they don't accurately express heartfelt honor from us for doing the right thing. Words of affirmation, opportunities and extra privileges can all become part of the reward system that helps build a correct value system in our homes. We must give attention to what is right and celebrate it well. Reward also helps create emotional currency with our kids so that we are able to bring correction when it is needed. Our daughter, Leah, needed very little correction throughout her years as a child. The reason was that she was deeply affected by her desire not to disappoint us as her mom and dad. For her, this showed a very healthy respect and was an act of honor that was not required of her. It was inside her early in life.

Generational Responsibility

One of my all-time favorite quotes is from one of the Founding Fathers of the United States, John Adams. He was the nation's first vice president, serving under George Washington, and he became the second president of the United States. Adams was a brilliant man with a deep understanding of the political process and the progressive nature of society. His quote speaks deeply to me:

> I must study politics and war that my sons may have liberty to study mathematics and philosophy. My sons ought to study mathematics and philosophy, geography, natural history, naval architecture, navigation, commerce and agriculture, in order to give their children a right to study painting, poetry, music, architecture, statuary, tapestry and porcelain.*

*Founders Online, "John Adams to Abigail Adams, 12 May 1780," *National Archives*, https://founders.archives.gov/documents/Adams/04-03-02-0258#AFC03d260n4 (spellings updated).

I guess the reason this statement moves me so much is that it contains wisdom for how the priority of one generation is to make room for greater liberty and freedom for the following generation. It is the heart of God for us to live for a generation we will never see. For me, this quote contains the conceptual insight needed to fulfill this task. The only warning I have concerning this understanding is that the following generations have to become aware of the price paid for their freedom. But even that is not a magic pill. It must produce thankfulness in them, or they will become entitled and will then use their freedom as a license for excess in all things.

It is the responsibility of one generation to set the stage for the increase and blessing of the next. But the blessing cannot be material only. It must be a blessing of character, insight and thankfulness. We have the responsibility to train our children beyond knowledge and into character. With that thought in mind, when Eric turned eighteen, I wrote him a letter that listed the "10 Things I Wanted My Children to Know" before they left home. The letter represented my commitment toward Brian and Leah as well, of course, and it embodied my goals for *intentional parenting*. I include the letter for you as appendix 1 in the back of this book.

Training at Home

The instruction in Deuteronomy about parents teaching their children became so strong for our Weaverville church family that we started working on training parents to deliberately train children in their homes. In fact, we eventually created Sunday school in the home. Every parent was the teacher of the class. Of course, the children were encouraged to bring their neighborhood friends home for this as well.

Initially we ordered a teacher's manual for every household. Eventually we made our own curriculum so a parent with a sixteen-year-old young person and a five-year-old child would not have to have two separate lessons. We organized it so that the subject would be the same for both, but the project associated with the lesson and the application would be more age specific. I had a team of people help me create the material that we passed around to every household.

The point is, we were intentional and purposeful, with a goal of teaching the Gospel, values, relationships and life skills. And while this may seem different from the "as you do life" approach I mentioned earlier, both are valuable, with unique fruit of their own. (For those interested in pursuing this concept further, I have provided a "Home Sunday School Parent's Guide" as appendix 2.)

Our Values *thoughts, values, beliefs, and actions*

The following are what I call the four cornerstones of thought. They set the parameters for our thoughts, values, beliefs and actions. These are the things that shape culture when they are put into practice. I deal with them more thoroughly in my book *The Way of Life* (Destiny Image, 2018), but here I will include as appendix 3 a wonderful declaration that our children's ministry created from my teaching on this subject. We use it for both adults and children. The young people who attend Bethel Christian School are also taught it. Adopting these values will have great effect on the home, and through us, these values will affect the world around us.

God Is Good

God's goodness cannot be exaggerated. It can be diluted, twisted and redefined. But it is impossible for us to exaggerate this trait of His. Because He is better than we think, we must change the way we think. His goodness allows and inspires us to *dream big.*

Nothing Is Impossible

Everything God made has limitations. But He does not. In wanting us to share in this unfathomable reality, He said, "Nothing is impossible for those who believe. Because of this reality, and the privilege we have in co-laboring with Him, we must *take risks* to see what He might do.

Everything Was Settled at the Cross

There is nothing that Jesus left out when He died in our place on the cross. His blood paid for everything. Every issue, for all eternity, was settled at Calvary. Because I am serving the One who thought of everything, I must *trust Him* when things look different from what I expected or believed for.

I Am Important

Every person is significant. There are no "throwaways." I am to love my neighbor as I love myself,—so it must be important for us to love ourselves, recognizing our personal significance in God's eyes. No one who knows who God made him or her to be would want to be anyone else. This reality must inspire us to *serve well*, for in God's Kingdom, greatness is seen in serving well.

Children Hear

Moments ago, Beni and I returned home after receiving prayer from a group of about twenty ten-year-olds. They told us what they felt God was saying to us. It was beautiful and so encouraging. If we are going to train our children to hear from God and represent Him, we must give them the occasion to practice what they have learned. This is essential as they learn to seek God for the direction they will take in life. You will also be amazed how much this will add to your faith, giving the clarity of God's heart to yours.

This practice of hearing God and speaking is important for children to do as they learn to love and serve others. In fact, one of the most important parts of our leadership conference is the prophetic ministry over every participant. Several years ago, we started adding a child to each team. And it is often the eight-year-old who will speak the most profound word over a grown-up leader.

Start early in creating an environment for your children where they will expect to hear from the Lord. Everybody can hear from God. Don't make it spooky, weird, strange or out of reach. Make it common, and make it simple. Give your kids decisions to make. Have them pray about something. Create in them an appetite to hear the Lord by talking with them about how it works in your life. For example, bring up in conversation, "I had this impression today, and here's what happened."

When you talk about a miracle that takes place because you had an impression that you paid attention to, it not only trains your kids in how God speaks; it also creates an appetite for God to speak. Instill in them the expectation to hear from God, and teach them your own personal skills. Then ask them, "What do you think God would be saying in this situation?" Don't ask, "What did God tell you?" until they have a history. Just ask them what they think, what their opinion is. Get that and weigh it, which is a great way to develop the hearing skill in them.

If we believe that God can use children, we must make room for their involvement in our efforts to love and minister to people. Learning to empower kids, within our guidance, is vital in order for them to become all that God designed them to be—giant-killers who shape the course of world history.

4

Ruling and Serving in the Home

GOVERNMENT MAY SEEM like an ill-fitting subject for a book on raising children, but I would like to suggest that it is not. At least, it is not, when you consider what government is. It is the God-given responsibility to manage something. Government is a human institution created by God, to represent God. It is never for the sake of the person in charge.

Parents are governmental representatives of God, as *family* is the first institution God created. As a Father, God fashioned the family and its natural bent toward unity after Himself—*Father, Son and Holy Spirit*. God is the perfect model of harmony and unity. When Adam and Eve were created, they represented the Godhead in miniature through their relationship, unity and responsibilities. They were family. They had purpose.

Whenever a person has a responsibility to govern, he or she has an obligation to find out how that authority is to be expressed. God understands both the need for leadership and how proper leadership brings benefit to those who are being led. He also understands the tragedies that take place under ungodly leadership. The Old

Testament kings bring enough examples of how to do leadership wrong to last us a lifetime.

All institutions need government. It really does not matter if that governmental position is the president of a nation, the CEO of a corporation, the pastor of a church or the parents in a home; all these roles are essential for the success and advancement of the institutions they lead. And all government serves two basic purposes: *to protect and to empower*. Those purposes are best accomplished by people who know when and how to rule, and when and how to serve.

Servants Rule, Rulers Serve

Many Christians are aware of Jesus' teaching about becoming the least and serving well. At the same time, many tend to be ignorant of the fact that we also have the responsibility to rule. An example is when the apostle Paul gave instructions for elders. He stated, "The elders who *rule well* are to be considered worthy of double honor, especially those who work hard at preaching and teaching" (1 Timothy 5:17, emphasis added). The whole theme of wisdom in Proverbs has its roots in this concept. The word *proverb* comes from a word that means "to reign." The point is, wisdom enables us to rule over the issues of life in a way that represents the King and His Kingdom.

Some fail at ruling because they don't want to make hard decisions. Avoiding responsibility sometimes falls under the guise of being a servant. We serve best when we understand the authority we carry. We are to rule with the heart of a servant, and serve with the heart of a king. *Ruling with the heart of a servant* means we lead with humility, making sure we use our authority for the benefit of others. *Serving with the heart of a king* is to serve with confidence, knowing we must draw upon the unlimited resources of the King we serve. Once again, it is an expression of humility, with a backbone of confidence, that enables us to draw upon God's resources as needed to serve effectively. If we don't see our need to draw upon God's unlimited resources, both in the natural and spiritual realms, we have failed to see the assignment that lies before us. In seeing my responsibility, I become hungry enough for breakthrough that I seek Him with no other options in mind.

Perhaps another reason for believers resisting the idea of ruling is that we have seen so many examples of people doing so with self-promotion and selfish interests in mind. They use their position for their own sake, not to benefit those around them. This misuse of authority and responsibility complicates the issue, as God intended rulers to rule, as evidenced in both the Old and New Testaments. The basic premise of authority is that we have been given a tool to use for the sake of others in representing the nature and heart of God. This often means we speak on behalf of those who have little or no voice. That is one of the purest forms of our use of authority in His name.

Rarely can those being led pay back for the services done for them. We all despise the concept of government leaders receiving financial kickbacks under the table from businesses or other leaders because they used their authority to favor them unfairly. And yet, it is common for adults to misuse their authority in the home to make themselves feel powerful.

The misuse of the authority to rule has caused many to reject the concept of ruling. But this is merely a reaction to error, not a response to what God says in His Word. Instead of avoiding responsibility or abusing our authority, let's learn how to use authority correctly and represent Him well. When He is represented well, He is manifested more clearly.

Jesus was the ultimate example of serving and ruling. He washed the disciples' feet in service. But He also exercised authority over demons and disease. He gave instructions and commands on how people should live their lives. He challenged the crowds with correction and insight. His leadership was perfect in that He both ruled and served. Knowing when and how is key. This is especially true for parents. How we navigate this responsibility illustrates to our children the adventure we have with God.

Kings Were God's Idea

Israel asked to have a king like the nations had that surrounded them. This was a tragic season in Israel's history, since they were rejecting God's leadership and direct involvement in their everyday affairs. God warned them about the consequences:

> So Samuel spoke all the words of the LORD to the people who had asked of him a king. He said, "This will be the procedure of the king who will reign over you: he will take your sons and place them for himself in his chariots and among his horsemen and they will run before his chariots. He will appoint for himself commanders of thousands and of fifties, and some to do his plowing and to reap his harvest and to make his weapons of war and equipment for his chariots. He will also take your daughters for perfumers and cooks and bakers. He will take the best of your fields and your vineyards and your olive groves and give them to his servants. He will take a tenth of your seed and of your vineyards and give to his officers and to his servants. He will also take your male servants and your female servants and your best young men and your donkeys and use them for his work. He will take a tenth of your flocks, and you yourselves will become his servants. Then you will cry out in that day because of your king whom you have chosen for yourselves, but the LORD will not answer you in that day."
>
> Nevertheless, the people refused to listen to the voice of Samuel, and they said, "No, but there shall be a king over us, *that we also may be like all the nations, that our king* may judge us and go out before us and *fight our battles.*"
>
> 1 Samuel 8:10–20, emphasis added

God knew the hearts of men and knew how their kings would use their power to serve themselves. Without the influence of God on the human heart, power tends to be a tool for self-promotion, personal pleasure, comfort and more wealth. Leaders who use power in this way expand their personal kingdom at the expense of others. Here is the downfall of governments all over the world: Government increases, while the significance of the individual decreases. This is not biblical government.

Look at Israel's reasoning for wanting a king. They wanted to be like other nations. They also wanted a leader who would take their individual responsibility as citizens and fight their battles for them. Whenever we give personal responsibility away, it will cost us in the long run. It certainly did for Israel.

Our homes are no different. If we fail to understand the God-given responsibilities for our own household, we will continue to forfeit our role to institutions and governments in ways that God never intended. In recent years, more and more of the authority for the home has been given to government, and even to corporations. And we are paying for it in significant ways, as the family is being redefined into something so far away from God's original design and intent. Today's governmental definition of family is becoming frighteningly dissimilar to the Creator's creation.

When God spoke to Abram about his future, He stated that kings would come from his descendants: "I will make you exceedingly fruitful, and I will make nations of you, and kings will come forth from you" (Genesis 17:6). Here God states that He intended for there to be kings. But He wanted kings raised up in His time, with His heart. David was such a king. He could be trusted with power because he was in pursuit of God's heart and purpose.

Our success at home is connected to our commitment to mirroring David's pursuit. We are kings in our homes. As such, we bear the responsibility to pursue God's heart, which ensures that we do not use the position for our own sake and purposes. But the assignment does not end there, as we also have the privileged challenge, as parents, of raising royalty.

Historically, often when the thought of raising royalty comes to mind, spoiled and entitled children are what we picture. There is reason for such concern, since the nature of man without Christ has a strong leaning in that direction. But consider what would be accomplished if we succeeded in what might seem politically incorrect—raising children with a sense of royal responsibility, who have confidence in their God-given commission.

Imagine what it would be like if our children were raised with the dignity, grace, humility and awareness of the incredible resources at their disposal to use for the sake of others.

Protect and Empower

As I already said, all government has two basic responsibilities—to protect and to empower. The words that represent these two ideas may change, but their impact is similar. Peter addressed this basic concept of governing by describing two unique expressions of it—to punish wrongdoers and to praise those who do right:

> Submit yourselves for the Lord's sake to every human institution, whether to a king as the one in authority, or to governors as sent by him for the *punishment* of evildoers and the *praise* of those who do right.
>
> 1 Peter 2:13–14, emphasis added

The effect of these two actions encourages and rewards good over evil. The one role of those who govern creates protection, and the other fuels the hearts of those who give themselves for the betterment of society—the builders.

Paul dealt with the same subject in Romans, where once again we see the same concept connected to government:

> For rulers are not a cause of fear for good behavior, but for evil. Do you want to have no fear of authority? Do what is good and *you will have praise* from the same; for it is a minister of God to you for good. But if you do what is evil, be afraid; for it does not bear the sword for nothing; for it is a minister of God, an avenger who *brings wrath* on the one who practices evil.
>
> Romans 13:3–4, emphasis added

Praise is what encourages and empowers. Wrath is the justice element that restores the standard for a society by causing fear of wrong-doing. Justice done correctly protects us.

Many believers have been ignoring the mandate for righteousness in government that is established when our leaders have the courage to enforce justice. These believers quote as their reason Jesus' mandate to forgive those who have wronged us. His instruction for our personal lives in this respect keeps us from the torment of bitterness and is an extremely liberating way to live. But He was not describing how civil government should work. That instruction is found throughout the Bible, revealing the need for justice. The governmental leaders who make these difficult decisions are called *ministers of God*. This is not meant to exclude the privilege of mercy, yet it is justice that creates the confidence in society that all will work out well.

I want to use one more example of ruling and serving that I find fascinating from the book of Nehemiah. The name Nehemiah means *comforter*. He is often a type of the Holy Spirit, as he enabled the people of God to rebuild the walls of Jerusalem in weeks, when they had been trying for decades.

> From that day on, half of my servants carried on the *work* while half of them held the *spears*, the shields, the bows and the breastplates; and the captains were behind the whole house of Judah. Those who were rebuilding the wall and those who carried burdens took their load with one hand *doing the work* and the other *holding a weapon*. As for the *builders*, each wore his *sword* girded at his side as he built, while the trumpeter stood near me.
>
> Nehemiah 4:16–18, emphasis added

This is such a beautiful picture of the concept of a healthy and purposeful government. Nehemiah, a representative of the king, was sent to direct the rebuilding of Jerusalem. But his assignment was unpopular with the surrounding nations. He built in the midst of opposition. For this reason, the workers were to be protected or have weapons to protect themselves. The two concepts of *protecting* and *empowering* are clearly manifested in this example of governmental responsibility. And whether or not we are building cities or parenting our children, we face opposition. There are many who would like to impose their will on us as we raise our children with divine purpose. Once again, we were born into a war. The conflict is over the destiny of our children.

These verses from Nehemiah illustrate this point perfectly. One half of the workers built, while the other half protected. And then there was the group who did both at the same time—they built with one hand and carried a weapon in the other. And then there was the last group of workers, who built with a sword at their side. The point is, they *protected*, and they *empowered* the building to go forward.

Builders Unite!

As parents and grandparents, we are architects and builders. We both protect and empower. God has made us to be the tools in His hands, who shape the values, character, gifts and thoughts of a generation. Our children are being uniquely positioned to represent God in the earth. Courage, with the mind of Christ, is essential to be successful. To do our part well, we must always have a weapon in hand as we prayerfully protect the lives of the ones we are building up and empowering.

5

Architects and Designers

W E ARE BUILDERS of families, individuals and legacies, as I
said earlier. When we have an idea of what we are building, and when we are willing to pay the price to use the
highest-quality building blocks, the reward of our efforts will be great.

The building blocks of a healthy home are many. In this chapter, we
will look at some of the building blocks that I consider to be the most
important ones. Let's start with the greatest building block of all, love.

Love

As governmental agents representing God Himself, we are required
to build something in and through our children's lives that represents Him well. Truly, the greatest of all building materials for our
homes is love. God's love, the rarest of all loves, gives and requires
nothing in return. "Love" is easy to write down on paper, but much
harder to practice. Yet it is the heart and soul of a home that raises
giant-killers.

Love is the most essential building block for the home. It is the
cornerstone. We see the greatest example of love in the sacrifice of

Jesus on the cross. He laid down His life for His friends (see John 15:13). But the best working definition of love is found in Paul's first letter to the Corinthian Church:

> Love is patient, love is kind and is not jealous; love does not brag and is not arrogant, does not act unbecomingly; it does not seek its own, is not provoked, does not take into account a wrong suffered, does not rejoice in unrighteousness, but rejoices with the truth; bears all things, believes all things, hopes all things, endures all things.
>
> 1 Corinthians 13:4–7

Any family that lives by this standard will experience things others only dream of. God trusts those who give themselves to His purpose with such clarity of heart and mind. This love, which requires nothing in return, is called *perfect love*. It is God's love. Living with love, the cornerstone of behavior, sets the boundaries for life.

The husband is responsible for the standard of love in the home. Husbands are to love their wives as Jesus loved the Church and gave Himself for her. That is the only standard worth following. In doing so, we find that the high-water mark of sacrificial love sets a standard for the household that is hard to ignore in tough seasons. Interestingly, the Ephesians 5 passage on husbands and wives says for the husband to love his wife, but it commands the wife to respect her husband. Why is there no command to love? As it pertains to our relationship with Jesus, 1 John 4:19 says, "We love, because He first loved us." His love for us is what equips us to love Him in return, with perfect love. This principle can be applied to the home. When the husband loves sacrificially, the wife and children have little problem loving in return.

Peace

On the other hand, the wife is the one responsible for the atmosphere of the home. I realize that in many homes both parents now work, so that standard may seem impractical. But even when Beni was working, our approach was that she was the primary contributor to the atmosphere. And I protected Beni and her role. Taking this outlook helped us immeasurably, and our home became a place of sacrificial love and extraordinary peace. An atmosphere of peace is another important building block of a healthy home.

Atmosphere is a presence-based value. That means that we learned as Mom and Dad to host the Spirit of God in our home. We worked hard never to violate His abiding presence, as He was and is our greatest treasure. His heart is violated in two primary ways:

1. Grieving Him. "Do not grieve the Holy Spirit of God" (Ephesians 4:30).
2. Quenching Him. "Do not quench the Spirit" (1 Thessalonians 5:19).

We grieve Him with wrong attitudes, thoughts, behavior, values and plans. We quench Him when we do not respond to His leading and empowering presence. One is when we do wrong, and the other is when we fail to do right. His abiding presence always enables us to do what He commands, so we are without excuse.

Adoration and affection for Him draw Him close. As we maintain this value of affection for Him, our lives, homes and workplaces all come under the beautiful influence of the living God. Learning how to live with that supreme value is paramount in having a home of peace.

These two building blocks, the principles of sacrificial love and a peaceful atmosphere, are just that—principles we live by. Keep in mind that the instructions for the husband to love sacrificially and the wife to influence the atmosphere are functions that both actually share. The wife loves, and the husband contributes to the atmosphere. But having an understanding of our primary contributions as husband and wife helped Beni and me immensely in building a home for Christ.

Principles

When the values of the Kingdom of God shape how we think and what we have an appetite for, we know they have truly taken root in our hearts. These values are what we refer to as Kingdom principles. Learning to identify and understand these principles helps us be more intentional in living within the realm of His dominion, and they also help us better communicate the wisdom of God to others.

Consider this: Solomon was the wisest person ever to live, apart from Jesus Christ, of course. He asked for wisdom because of his responsibility as king. He recognized that he was unable to lead the people of God correctly without divine wisdom. This is also the correct position of every parent alive. Our responsibility is beyond our natural ability. The challenge involved in parenting is exponentially more difficult in our day, when you consider the spirit of the day we live in. This should become the motivation for all of us to come before God and humbly ask for wisdom. Thankfully, the intense evil of the day is no match for the wisdom and power of God.

I have determined to live here on earth as it is in heaven. That means that as it is in heaven, so my number one value is for the presence of God. Turning my affection toward Him through the day, and even in the night, anchors me in the greatest reality in existence. But there are times when that "felt presence" is not there. Notice the term "felt presence." He will never leave us or forsake us, so He is always there. But there are times when He shuts down our ability to be aware of His presence. He does this to see what we will do with what we know. He did it to Hezekiah: "God left him alone only to test him, that He might know all that was in his heart" (2 Chronicles 32:31). It is never punishment. But He will test us to see how we respond to His will when the inspiration is gone. His will is revealed in Scripture. It is vital to have a people on the earth who will obey Him when they feel like it and when they don't.

Such moments are difficult but vital, as they determine how much of the glory we are able to carry. God's desire is for us to live and thrive under the weightiness of His presence into all the earth. But if we have the bent to obey only when we feel good, or if we take the glory to ourselves for His answers, we cannot be trusted with what He has in mind for us.

It is for this reason we must learn the principles of the Kingdom of God. Turning to them in these moments means we understand what is important and valuable to Him, even when inspiration is gone. This may seem like a strange topic to bring up, but this is why praising Him in difficult times is so important. By giving Him thanksgiving and praise when things are difficult, we develop the "faith muscle" that enables us to live and see beyond our immediate emotional state. Those who learn this can be trusted with more. Teaching this to our children is essential, as we are raising them to be carriers of the glory into the earth. There will be a generation who will yield to and dwell in the glory of God. It might as well be our children!

Endurance

No pain, no gain. This phrase used in weightlifting is also useful in life. Muscles get sore in exercise. If you are not willing to work through the pain, there will be little development or growth of the muscle you are exercising. Character and faith are also developed in this way.

Living intentionally helps us weather the painful decisions, because there is gain on the other side. I cannot think of any area of life where this is truer than in raising children. The journey is littered with painful decisions. Sometimes the most pain is found in trying to be consistent, when it would be much easier to compromise in order to lessen the discomfort of a moment.

There is something greater than the *pain*. It is the *gain*. The pain is temporary. The gain is eternal. If this were not true, the pain would not be worth it. We endure because the reward is greater. Much greater. It is a great bonus to see children grow up in our homes to represent an aspect of God's nature in an honest and wholesome way. This helps create legacy. And legacy cannot be overrated. King

David left a mark on God's heart that was so significant that several hundred years later, God treated people with an increased measure of favor because they were David's descendants. That is remarkable. Touching the heart of God with our faithfulness and creating a legacy that favors multiple generations should be the goal of every believing household.

Presence is passion. Principle is discipline. We were never meant to be known for our discipline. We are meant to be known for our passion. But having the principles of His Kingdom deeply embedded in our understanding helps us navigate the seasons when inspiration is lacking.

Outside Christ, people perform to create an identity so that they might be accepted. The longing of everyone's heart is to belong. It is vital. But in Christ, things are different. We start out accepted by God. From that place of acceptance, our identity is formed. And it is out of our identity that we perform. When we model and teach that approach to life, it will enable our children to skip years of unnecessary crisis and engage fully with who God made them to be.

Hope

Hope is the easy-to-identify characteristic of any parent who lives under the influence of the Holy Spirit. It really is the heartbeat of heaven, and as such, it must become the heartbeat of the home. God is not depressed, worried or fearful. When we are those things, it is apparent that His influence in us has diminished. He has hope. I know He is God, and as God, He is in charge. So there is reason for His hope. But are we not in Christ? Isn't it true that nothing is impossible for God, but also that nothing is impossible for those who believe? Isn't it true that His promises are more than sufficient for anything we could possibly face?

When I am hopeless, I am reminded that I have stepped out of my call and design, having forgotten what He has said and promised. In those moments, I must confess and repent my way back to my proper position, until hope is restored. Any area of our life for which we have no hope is under the influence of a lie. Learning to recognize hopelessness enables us to address whatever would undermine our health and well-being as a family.

One of my favorite hope stories of all time comes from the discoveries of Johns Hopkins scientist Curt Paul Richter. In the 1950s, he performed experiments on rats in which he discovered that they could swim in high-sided buckets of circulating water for only about 15 minutes in order to stay alive. After that, they would give up and sink. But when the swimming rats were rescued briefly and then put back in the water, they managed to swim for 60 hours. That was 240 times longer than rats that were not temporarily rescued. How was that possible? Dr. Richter concluded that it was because the rescued rats were given hope. The hope that they could be rescued again fueled their energy to keep swimming.

Character

Everything we teach our children has greater authority when we model it first in our own lives. If I require something from my child, it must be found in my life first. This is true in many areas worthy of discussion here, but for now, consider these important areas:

- I cannot expect my children to have a hunger for God's Word if they don't see me hunger for it. They must see me read it for myself. Don't just read the Word of God when you are in bed at night, away from your children. I am not saying we should put on a show to impress them. But we must put certain things on display so that our children are more likely to follow them. The same is true with your prayer life.

- Include your children in the privilege of giving. Give them money or possessions for the sole purpose of giving. Offerings at church are great places to start. But also give to the person waiting outside the grocery store, who needs help with food or gas money. Perhaps you can make it a talking point when you are driving home from the store. Stir up compassion in your kids. Let them see and participate in it at an early age.

- Compliment the individuals of your household in front of each other. Giving honor in the open had great dividends in our household. But in the presence of your children, also include giving honor to those outside your family. You can develop this way of thinking by asking them, "What do you like about . . .?" Mention the name of one of their friends, or perhaps one of yours. The point is, get them thinking about the character found in other people.

- Repent quickly and openly. If I treat someone rudely in front of my children, it is vital that I clean up my mess with an apology. This must be to the one I offended, as well as to my children who saw my unacceptable behavior. They must see my tenderness toward the Lord, and toward them. Don't use that kind of opportunity for a message on how your children ought to live. Simply be the example you want them to follow.

- Patience is one of the more necessary virtues in raising children. Oftentimes, parents become so frustrated with a child acting like a child that they take the opportunity to "preach" their message about being responsible. Often, it is merely verbal impatience disguised as training. My patience with my children nudges them to be patient with others.

- Serving is taught by doing. The role of the servant is the highest role in God's Kingdom. Illustrating that role is critical to training your children, or else they will want the entire world to rotate around them.

Purpose

Parents have the wonderful privilege of training children to know their identity, their purpose and their destiny. In reality, we were born to enjoy God. Perhaps it could better be said that we are *designed* to discover and enjoy the One who delights in us. That is perhaps what the enemy of our soul fears most—a people who love, enjoy and delight in God.

Part of our design is to be the eternal dwelling place of God. I don't know that there could be a more significant purpose, considering that the God of the universe longs to live in us. We are called the house of God. Learning to recognize His presence, as well as yield to His abiding Holy Spirit, are essential practices for those discovering their reason for being.

As His purposes become more and more pronounced in our children and ourselves, we have the unique privilege of representing God. I like to say *re*-presenting Jesus, because we have the distinct responsibility to manifest Him as He is. I am assuming that learning how to do this well takes a lifetime, as I still feel like a beginner. Yet I don't have the authority to change the assignment to something I feel I can do better. This is who we are and why we are here. People need to and should be able to see Jesus in and through us.

So then, we represent God in how we live and love, and in the same way, we reveal God. Jesus taught us, "Let your light shine before men in such a way that they may see your good works, and glorify your Father who is in heaven" (Matthew 5:16). As we reveal God for who He is, people will automatically be drawn to Him and will in turn glorify Him. This is the great privilege and responsibility of all of us. And this is what we must communicate to our young giant-killers.

6

Being a First Responder

JESUS DID NOT LIVE in reaction to the devil. Instead, He responded to the Father. This sets a biblical standard for all our lives, as God's will is for us not to react to something wrong, but to respond to what is right. It illustrates God's will when we respond rather than react. Understanding this will help each of us in all our relationships, but it is an especially practical approach to family life.

If there ever were passages of Scripture that captured the essence of God's nature as it pertains to all relationships in the Kingdom, it would have to be these two:

> Love is patient, love is kind and is not jealous; love does not brag and is not arrogant, does not act unbecomingly; it does not seek its own, is not provoked, does not take into account a wrong suffered, does not rejoice in unrighteousness, but rejoices with the truth; bears all things, believes all things, hopes all things, endures all things.
>
> Love never fails.
>
> 1 Corinthians 13:4–8

> Do nothing from selfishness or empty conceit, but with humility of mind regard one another as more important than yourselves; do

not *merely* look out for your own personal interests, but also for the interests of others. Have this attitude in yourselves which was also in Christ Jesus.

Philippians 2:3–5

These passages are relational masterpieces. While the first passage, part of the Love Chapter written to the Corinthian Church, is the high-water mark on the subject of what real love looks like, it is the latter passage that has affected my thinking. For me, in this Scripture the apostle Paul illustrated the down-to-earth application of the principles he discussed in the Love Chapter. In Philippians 2 he deals with the posture of the mind in viewing others correctly—*as more important than ourselves*. It has the discipline of embracing the *interests of others*, followed by the exhortation to embrace this as an overriding *attitude*—the same one Jesus had. This tells me that this is to be much more than an isolated action. Through practice, it can and must become our most natural response to a challenge or opportunity.

Our Approach

Beni and I made an agreement early in our marriage that we would never greet each other negatively when one or the other of us comes home from a long day. Unless there was an emergency, we never greeted each other at the door with a problem. Even if the kids had been acting up and needed a "meeting" with their dad, Beni's and my greeting was always warm and positive.

To be frank, some people don't want to go home when they are through with work. They don't know what they are going to get when they walk through the door. Will it be yelling, verbal abuse or an unloading of problems that have built up during the day? Rather than going home, many people go to the bar, work late or find some other activity to fill their time at the end of their day. The thought of walking into pain and conflict has a subconscious effect on people's schedules and priorities. With the kind of careless approach to life where we greet each other with negativity, we train our spouses not to want to come home or regroup at the end of the day.

When there are difficulties that need to be discussed, set up a mutually convenient time. If one spouse has dwelt on a problem all day and the other has not given the issue a second thought, it is really unfair to unload when the first person is ready to talk. Having respect for the other person might look something like this: "When you left the house this morning, it felt as if you ignored my attempt to get your help on a matter. I know you probably didn't mean it, but it has bothered me all day. Can we sit down later tonight, after the children are in bed, and talk through this for my sake?" I can never promise the conversation will always go well, but this approach of respect and honor puts the advantage in your favor.

I had a friend who went deer hunting. Just as he pulled the trigger to harvest his game, he noticed another hunter on the other side of the deer, also trying to shoot it. My friend shot the animal, while the other hunter accidently shot him. He lived to tell the story, but the lesson has always helped me illustrate the importance of facing challenges together.

If a husband and wife, or parents and children, face a problem separately from each other, there is always the chance that the other family member will be the one who gets *shot*, so the speak. But if a husband and wife will stand side by side in facing an issue, they can together address the problem with much less likelihood of one wounding the other. Giving one another the benefit of the doubt is a great place to start.

The Communications War

Communication does not have to be warlike. It never has been that way for Beni and me. We have too much respect for each other to treat each other as an enemy or as the target in dealing with a problem. I call the communications issue a war because this is where the powers of darkness work so hard to divide us. All of us. Succeeding in our communications, and teaching our children to do the same, sets us up for increased favor, increased success and a happy life in a community of trusted family members and friends.

Teaching children the art of good communication begins in the home. It must involve processing disagreement and pain. Here are some ideas on this beautiful subject that have helped Beni and me succeed in this area with our family:

- Be an example of how to communicate well. Good communication is not just getting your point across. It has a primary focus on understanding the people you are talking to. Husbands and wives set the stage for their children in this matter. The kids will follow your lead. Speaking down to someone in an insulting way or mocking a person is taboo, as it drives that person away from you.

- Good communication happens when people don't feel threatened for having their opinion. Not reacting to our spouse or our children goes a long way in training for this desirable virtue.

- Speak the truth in love (see Ephesians 4:15). Speaking truth is critical, but only in the context of love. Love honors, values and celebrates the other person. This is communication.

- Model humility by confessing your mistakes. When the whole family sees the blunder, confess to the whole family. For example, raising your voice, being impatient or yelling at another driver are things that you can confess and then have prayed over by the whole family.

- Show concern for any family member who is discouraged or downcast. Respect that he or she may not want to talk right then. Honor the person by giving him or her some space to process, but show loving support. Some children have a very difficult time talking about their feelings. It is a continual challenge for parents since we tend to want our kids to talk most when they feel least like doing so. Learn to draw out your children's feelings when something has been exciting or fun, instead of only when there is a problem. It is easier to develop those skills at communicating feelings when there is not the pressure of disappointment or failure to deal with.

- It is often good to repeat what the other person has said in your own words, to make sure you understand. I used to encourage this in marriage counseling. It was painfully funny to see how often spouses were worlds apart, even though they were attempting to repeat what was just said by the other person only two minutes earlier. When there is great conflict, people read their bias or bitterness into what someone else just said. By repeating things back to others, you give them the chance to correct your perspective, and they can also see that you are interested in them.

- Stay away from assuming you know another person's motives. That one skill would save us tons of heartache and protect us from causing division. Learning to do that as parents, and then helping our children develop that ability, will work wonders for them in their lifetime. The Bible says of God, "You alone know the hearts of all the sons of men" (1 Kings 8:39). To think that we know what God says we cannot know opens us up to great deception. There is a real devil who would love to give us his gift of suspicion, in order to increase division in our homes and friendships. It is best to stay clear of this and learn to give people the benefit of the doubt. If God warns you of someone to stay clear of, by all means do so. But you don't need to imagine things that God is not giving you access to.

- To *commune* is the goal of communication. That implies the experience of having a deep emotional or spiritual relationship. While that is not possible to have with every person, it should be our ambition to be an authentic lover of truth and of people in whatever measure God has provided for us. Good communication is not just a way we show value for our own opinion. That is venting, whether or not it is emotional. Communication, *to commune*, is as much about listening as it is about speaking. The most important people in our lives are family. Learn to commune there, and you will be a champion at it elsewhere.

- I learned from Beni to pray for an understanding heart. I heard her pray that prayer early in our lives as parents. It was brilliant. An understanding heart helps us not to read into a situation what is not there. It leads us away from being defensive, which almost always hurts the goal of communication.

- Good communication is more likely when we have great value for the person we are talking to. We are then less liable to be sharp or rude. My dad used to say, "When you wash the feet of another, you find out why they walk the way they do." Having a servant's heart helps communication succeed.

- Good communication takes time. Be spontaneous, but never put another person at a disadvantage in doing so. Learn to schedule a time to talk if necessary, as well as to respect the other person's plans. Communication is important enough sometimes to be a calendar item.

- Use humor. Laugh at yourself, but don't use humor to dishonor or ridicule. I have friends who use humor to criticize, and they think it does not hurt because the other person laughs. Much group laughter at criticism is pressured laughter, or is an attempt to show that people still have value for the critic. But that does not mean the humor was well received or valued. It significantly damages your credibility whenever you use humor to mock or hurt another person.

- A good communicator always builds an arena of safety for the other person to talk in. It means that the other person's opinion is important to me, as I value him or her as a person. This creates a nonthreatening atmosphere where the exchange of life becomes possible.

- People with good self-esteem seem to communicate better since they are not as likely to react to a misunderstanding. Their identity is not wrapped up in the other person's approval, and therefore they can weather challenging conversations better, without reacting. If I am to love others as I love myself, it stands to reason that I must love myself to love others well.

- Whenever one of our family members hurts another, he or she was always required to apologize. The ones apologizing were not allowed to say just the words "I'm sorry." They had to say what they were sorry for. In other words, they had to confess their sin to the other person: "I'm sorry I took your candy." The ones doing the forgiving could not say just the words "It's okay" or "I forgive you." They had to say, "I forgive you for taking my candy." If they refused or needed time, they were sent to their room to think it through. I would then go back to their bedroom after about ten minutes and help them walk through the process. Being specific helps with real repentance and healing. Their tone of voice was also critical to me. It had to be tender and responsive, not reactive and rude. Bitterness affects the container, not the target.

These are just a few of the principles we have tried to live by. It is well worth the time it takes to practice and develop strengths in these different areas of communication, as they will affect the rest of your children's lives.

One more thing I want to mention about communication is the widespread use of electronic devices today, which is more of an issue than it used to be. Kids, and in fact all of us, have so many more things to be involved with now—iPhones, tablets, computers, access to the Internet. I love all these tools. Playing on the phone can be recreational, and I even find it refreshing. These devices can be fun, but they can also distort values and create a narrow, nonsocial focus that hurts relationships and communication. It is wise to set some boundaries for yourself and your children in this area. No texting, no iPhones, no anything at the dinner table. Model it. When you converse with your children, give them your full attention and look them in the eyes. Don't be divided, looking at your phone, except if you have to make sure there is not an emergency. Teach your kids to communicate with others the same way, with the same level of respect. Use electronic tools with wisdom, making sure they remain tools that enhance life. Don't let them be in competition with relationships and family. Curtail the use of these things if you need to. Make sure you value people first, and monitor how well your kids are doing in life and how well they associate with people.

Interruptions with Purpose

On a number of occasions, my children would interrupt my conversation with another adult. Even though there were times that it could easily be frustrating, I would apologize to the adult and excuse myself for just a moment. I would then turn my attention to my child, who was (and still is) one of the four most important persons in my life. For example, if one of the boys interrupted us, I would ask him what he had to say and would then listen with great focus on him alone. He was usually interrupting to show me another lizard he had caught or the spoil from another equally great adventure, or how he had hurt his finger while playing. It was important to him, and as such, it was important to me.

I realize how different my approach is from the norm, but it is a difference worth highlighting here because it pays such dividends in the long run. It made my children feel valuable, while also teaching them to value honoring others. When my children interrupted me, I gave them my undivided attention until after I had either celebrated their latest conquest or attended to their pain. But then I would explain something about communication to them, without making them feel ashamed for coming to me. I would say something like this: "I'm so impressed that you caught that lizard. I'll bet he was hard to catch. Good job! It's very important to me to know what you're doing and how you're having fun. But you might have noticed that I was talking with my friend. I always want you to be able to come to me at any time, with anything, but if you think it can wait just a few minutes, next time I'd love to finish my conversation."

At the end of that kind of encounter, my children were reassured in knowing that they were the most important people to me in the world, and that as my son or daughter, they had access to me at any time. It was their right and privilege. But they also knew how I valued and loved to honor my friends, too. Here they got to learn how to honor their father's friends, which is a biblical principle found in Proverbs 27:10. They could then see how to help me be successful in that area of life, without missing out on their all-important conversation with Dad about their recently apprehended reptile.

Our Home—Safe and Fun

Beni was good at making our home a healthy and safe place—so good that our children loved bringing their friends home with them after school. They even did this when they were in high school, which must qualify as some sort of miracle. Beni was so warm and welcoming that our kids' friends would often prefer coming to our house to doing something else.

Beni also added another benefit to their lives: These teenagers, both boys and girls, could talk with her about anything, and they did. She always treated them with honor and respect, yet was brutally honest. Plus, she never reacted in shock to anything that was said, which made them feel valued and safe. This elevated her to a place of great influence with a group of young men and women who were otherwise disconnected from most adults. As a result of her strength, wisdom and grace, they asked her for input on many personal issues. It was beautiful to see.

Our homes are supposed to be places of healing, strength, connection, identity and recharging of our batteries emotionally, mentally and spiritually. The way we respond to each other helps solidify this as a reachable goal.

Expectations Rule

All three of our children attended a Christian school from preschool through eighth grade. I am so thankful we were able to have them do that, since it brought significant influence into their lives in a way that complemented what they received in our home. Interestingly, their classes had about four different grades in each one. I loved that. They were able to grow up in a very diverse atmosphere and not be so age restrictive.

Variety is essential to healthy development. This is especially true when children have the opportunity to grow up in an environment like our kids' school. At one age they were the youngest in the class, receiving help and input from the older kids. At another time they were the oldest, serving the younger children. This kind of practice is very positive in the long run. The children had both the responsibility of influencing others and the task of learning from others in the process. Their teachers were very positive, sacrificing greatly so that these children would grow up to become contributors to society.

My children knew that when they brought me a report card, I had expectations. First and foremost, I would look at the teacher's evaluation of their attitude. We learned early in their formative years that if we were able to bring correction to their hearts while their issue was still in attitude form, we often could prevent bad conduct. During a time of discipline, I would send them to their room until their attitude changed. When I came back to check on them, I expected them to deal with their heart and be tender again. If they were not doing so, then we took further measures.

My greatest concern for who my children were becoming was their respect toward their teacher, and then of course toward their fellow students. Attitude is paramount. Academics are important, but the heart is more important. Their teachers always graded them in the area of attitude, too, for which I was so thankful. It was brilliant. The kids watched as I opened first to that page of their report card, because they knew what mattered to me. As someone once stated, you must inspect what you expect. And so I did, and I honored them accordingly.

After checking the grade the children received for attitude, the second thing I looked at was their grade in Bible. Because it was a Christian school they were taught the Bible, for which I was also thankful. It was critical in my thinking that they understood the Scriptures. Not because I was a pastor. That never crossed my mind. It was for the benefit of the life ahead of them. I wanted them to be successful. And it is very difficult to be eternally successful without a foundation in the Word of God. I looked at that Bible grade with great interest.

When I was through with those two things, I would review the rest of the report card. I can truthfully say that if they got those two things right, the rest followed nicely. It really did work that way. As long as they were committed to keeping their heart issues right and were devoted to the Word of God, everything else fell into place. In reality, they could have received bad grades in several other subjects and I would have been as happy as ever, if the attitude of the heart and the Bible were good. For me, that is what it looks like to build with the big picture in mind. And if their giants are slain on the inside, children will be much better positioned to deal with the giants in society.

Skills versus Heart

Heart issues were always our primary focus in raising our children. Proverbs 4:23 has been a life verse for me for about 45 years: "Watch over your heart with all diligence, for from it flow the springs of life." It is of primary interest to God, too, as He found David "a man after My heart" (see Acts 13:22). That really is amazing. God knows the most famous giant-killer in world history for his heart. David had a heart for God's heart. This is brilliant!

Many years ago, my dad wanted to hire a music pastor. I was an associate at the time, and he kept the whole staff apprised of his progress. He needed someone with a knowledge of choirs, TV production, orchestra and much more. Dad brought highly qualified people to Redding from all over the country and spent time with them, interviewing them as possible candidates for the job. These were some of the top individuals in the country; they were highly skilled, with great ministries.

When it came time to make a decision, my dad met with the rest of the staff to tell us the outcome. I will never ever forget that conversation. He told us of the people he had brought to Redding to interview. He then told us he had chosen someone who was very musical, but who had never done any of the things we were asking him to do. Dad followed this somewhat shocking statement with, "But he has the same heart that we do."

My dad's approach was that skills could be taught, but heart is another matter altogether. He hired Bob Kilpatrick to be on our team, and Bob and his family remain very special friends to this day. It is all about the heart.

I learned something that day that has stayed with me as a beautiful example of the kind of values that influence good decisions. Skills are important, but they can be learned. Heart is greater than skills. This approach has remained our primary target in training our children and grandchildren.

Delegated Authority

It was important to me for my children to understand authority from God's perspective. If we are being pulled over for a traffic violation, we don't have the right to keep driving if we know that the officer is a horrible husband and father. We pull over because of the badge and uniform. He represents the law, and I must respect that.

Whenever we had a babysitter watch our children, or a school-teacher teach them at school, or a Little League coach help them with baseball, our children knew that those people were delegated authority. Delegated by me. To dishonor them was to dishonor me. For what it is worth, they also knew that they could violate that person's directives if those directives violated God's Word and direction for our family.

I remember that I had to teach this powerful lesson to our two little boys whom we cared for from the foster child agency. They had seen their dad abuse their mother, and they had much less respect for Beni than for me. When they were disrespectful, I would take them aside and tell them, "That is my wife. And you will not treat my wife that way!"

They then started to associate Beni's authority with mine. When necessary, I told that to my children as well. It is one of the ways you teach the concept of delegated authority. If the children were disrespectful to the babysitter, they were disrespectful to me. It was vital to instill that building block for life into how they see those who have authority in their lives.

I realize that we can easily name exceptions where one of these delegated individuals might want to violate a child or take part in some other illegal activity. Of course that is wrong, and no person has to submit to that nonsense. But most people's objection to authority has nothing to do with illegal or even unwise activity. They just disagree with the person put in authority.

We talk a lot about our core values, as those are the things that help define culture. To live them out well, there must be an understanding of authority in the Kingdom of God. There is a great story about a centurion who told Jesus that his servant was sick and dying (see Matthew 8:5–13; Luke 7:1–10). Jesus answered that He would come and heal him. The centurion said Jesus did not have to do that. All He had to do was speak the word, and the servant would be healed. And then the centurion explained that because he was a man under authority, those under him must likewise do what he said.

He got it! Being under the authority of God is what gives us authority over the issues of life that the works of darkness have damaged.

If you ever want to impress God, try moving in the kind of faith that is partnered with divine reasoning. This Roman soldier impressed Jesus in a remarkable way. He continued to explain himself: "Because I represent a higher authority, those under me will respond." That concept of authority is huge. It is so absent in our present culture, where there is so little value for authority. In the long run that hurts us, because we become unable to function the way Jesus did.

Powerful Children

Children need to be aware that they are powerful people who are able to make choices, and that they are not to be controlled by others. We want them to think for themselves, but we also want them to value the people whom God has put into their lives. This includes those with authority over them. Because children are powerful, they are able to be successful in honoring and yielding to authority, particularly when they first see in us the model of Kingdom authority put into practice.

As parents, it is also vital that in our relationships and communication we are first responders, not reactors. Being a first responder is just that—becoming the one who is first in responding to our children's needs, gifts and perceived purpose and call. When we model reacting, it teaches our children to avoid the challenges in life, while at the same time reinforcing the idea that they are always right and anyone who differs is wrong. When they see us respond to them and to others, it teaches them to value the person, as well as the issue at hand.

We model this approach to life in the way we treat our children. They will accomplish much more, and do it much sooner than most, if they can learn from us the beauty of giving a response to people instead of a reaction. It is the nature of a life of honor.

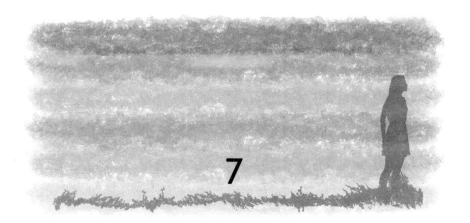

7

A Case for Godly Discipline

NO INSTITUTION is any stronger than its ability to discipline. It does not matter if we are talking about a nation, an organization or a family—discipline is vital. It is the other side of the coin whose face shows us the subject of reward. Without discipline, an entire culture is prone to entitlement and the resultant shame that accompanies unwise, unrestrained life choices. In this present day, we often raise children with little or no discipline, and then we complain about their lack of self-discipline. Those two realities are connected. The absence of external discipline leads to the absence of internal discipline.

Very few hot-button topics are more likely to get a reaction than the topic of discipline. There are some good reasons for this, and some pretty bad ones. A bad one is the social pressure, which should be completely meaningless to a real believer. The public is valued; public opinion is not. We will answer to the One for our choices. That is what matters.

A good reason for reacting against this subject is quite simply the fact that there has been so much abuse. Craziness exists in home after home, all in the name of discipline. Anger, violence and hatred surface. People who have never dealt with their own issues often take them out on their children. But reacting to the abuses of others never takes us to truth. Not using the tool of discipline is little better than abusing the tool of discipline. Both abuse and neglect have disastrous results. It is better that we give ourselves to finding the biblical standard and following it carefully.

Discipline comes from a heart of love, in an effort to shape the heart of a child with responsibility and purpose. God sets the standard for this area of our lives:

> It is for discipline that you endure; God deals with you as with sons; for what son is there whom *his* father does not discipline? But *if you are without discipline*, of which all have become partakers, then *you are illegitimate children* and *not sons*. Furthermore, we had earthly fathers to discipline us, and we respected them; shall we not much rather be subject to the Father of spirits, and live? For they disciplined us for a short time as seemed best to them, but *He disciplines us* for our good, *so that we may share His holiness. All discipline* for the moment seems not to be joyful, but *sorrowful*; yet to those who have been trained by it, afterwards *it yields the peaceful fruit of righteousness.*
>
> Hebrews 12:7–11, emphasis added

Read over these verses, giving special attention to the highlighted portions. The purpose and results of God's correction are so good. Our responsibility to discipline our children is patterned after this example. God corrects us because He loves us. Period. If He wanted to break or destroy us, it would take very little effort on His part. Venting His anger is never the goal, as His longsuffering is about a billion times bigger than our wildest imagination of longsuffering. Transformation is His target.

If God does not discipline us, we are illegitimate children. Illegitimate children don't have the same rights as real ones. The implications of this are staggering. God takes time with those who are His, working to build His character in them. But those whom He does not discipline are not His. In the same way that I would never discipline the neighborhood kids, likewise God does not deal with those who are not His. He gives His loving attention to those who belong to Him, as He longs to impart to them His *holiness* and the *peaceful fruit of righteousness*. Those are the results of receiving His correction.

To put this in a family context, discipline gives a child an identity, character and a purpose. We instill in our children an awareness of why we are alive and what our family has been given to do in the earth. Parents who don't discipline their children fail to give them the full impact of their inheritance and name.

Powerful Big People

Let me say at the onset that I believe in spanking. While many people react to my posture on this subject, saying that it is a barbaric way to raise a child, I believe it is a biblical way to deal with certain problems. It is not to be the only form of discipline, nor is it to be used in every situation. But it is one of the tools that will bring about godly results if used properly.

Spanking is not about the big people punishing the little people for not obeying their rules. It is not to give the adults the chance to vindicate themselves against these much smaller ones who have a will of their own. Proper discipline must be done in humility and in love, and the goal is to help refine the values and focus of the child.

I think most of us would agree that the real problem in this issue is the *spanker*. The abuses offered in the name of discipline have scarred a generation. But those raised without discipline (which includes spanking) have no compass. They lose the sense of direction and focus because they were left as a law unto themselves.

The following verse about *vision* is very well-known, and for good reason. But the most astonishing part of this Scripture is that it follows three verses on correction and discipline, which we will also discuss shortly. This verse gives us, in a sense, the result of growing up without correction: "Where there is no vision, the people are unrestrained, but happy is he who keeps the law" (Proverbs 29:18). Discipline, done correctly, helps refine purpose and vision in a person. It destroys the bent in a child for carelessness and floundering, and it brings godly restraints. It should never be done in anger. It is always meant for the child's benefit and well-being.

While spanking is not the only way to train our children, it is to be part of the toolkit that we use to shape them. To make sure that my heart was right in bringing that kind of correction to my kids, many times I sent them to their room while I took a few minutes to pray. I hated spanking them. There was never any pleasure. And while my pain was not in the same place as my children's pain, I still hurt deeply for them. I can honestly say that I did not spank my children in anger. I learned early on to respond and not react.

Discipline needs to be an occasion, not an outburst. Real discipline takes time. It is very easy to fail at this point since children never disobey at a convenient time. It may be when guests have come over to the house, or perhaps while we are at the grocery store. The point is, they usually know when and where they can get away with the most without suffering pain.

That means that we have to learn wisdom in dealing with our children, regardless of where we are. Being inconvenienced has caused many parents to move in anger, because a child can ruin an entire evening of having guests over to the house. Or some parents move to the other extreme and let a child disobey without reprisal. But if I don't respond when it is hard, that root of illegitimate independence will only grow deeper, requiring more serious actions later. Take the time needed to do things correctly. It will spare you disappointment and pain later on.

The Training We Never Intended

Many parents use emotional reactions that come out as anger and yelling to get their children to obey. Parents complain because a child does not listen, and they point out that it is only when they yell that the child responds. That is because the parent has trained the child that way.

Children learn that they don't always have to do what we say, because discipline does not follow their disobedience. It follows our anger. For example, if I tell Johnny to pick up his toys and he does not, then there needs to be some action on my end. The typical parent raises his or her voice after Johnny fails to do what he was told, telling him that he will be in trouble if he does not obey. Some parents will count to ten to give Johnny a chance to obey. This trains him to ignore directions, and instead, to respond to the buildup of anger or threats. And still, Johnny does not pick up the toys. It is only after a parent gets frustrated and yells that Johnny knows the loud words are about to be backed up with action.

This process teaches Johnny not to obey words, but instead, to obey our volume or emotional condition. He knows it always intensifies before we take action to back up what we commanded. Children want to avoid the act of discipline, if possible. The problem is, there is still foolishness bound up in a child's heart, and that must be dealt with. Kids want to have their own way for as long as they can. Our lack of action trains them to respond to emotion and not to words. Yet in most cases, one week of speaking calmly and giving instructions clearly will bring about a change in the home, if the parents' instructions are immediately followed with action. It does not take long to recalibrate a child to value what we say instead of reacting to our emotion.

It is important to realize that it is never too late to start parenting intentionally. If your kids are older (preteen and up) and you have not been an intentional parent, sit down and have an open conversation with them. Tell them, "I've not done what I should as a parent. I didn't know it, and now I'm trying to make changes because I believe in you kids, and I want you to succeed in life." And talk about setting new and necessary boundaries. Kids of any age have a built-in need for boundaries; they want to explore in safety. Try to come to some understanding of what works well for your kids at their current ages. Start with honor, and with reward for doing what is right, but make clear the consequences for doing what is wrong. Stack the deck with positive things, but set consequences for wrong decisions as well. And then respond to your children, rather than reacting emotionally as your default parenting method. It will change the atmosphere of your entire household.

My Personal Process for Discipline

Anytime discipline was in order in our home, it was my responsibility. I never wanted Beni to have to deal with that if I was home. This was my procedure:

- I would send my children to their room when discipline was called for. Depending on their age and attention span, I would give them anywhere from two to twenty minutes to think through what they had done wrong. During that time, I would pray to make sure I was in a place to correct for their sake and not mine. I wanted to improve their lives through discipline, not punish them.
- Then I would come into their room and discuss their wrong with them. There were times when I discovered that I had not communicated our expectations with them clearly. If that was the case, I would discuss the situation with them to make sure they now understood what was required of them. There was never any form of punishment in that situation. But following that moment, I would make sure to look for a change in their behavior once we left the room.
- If it was an issue of the heart, like a bad attitude, I would give them time to fix it while they were in their room. If I felt their repentance was genuine, we would join the rest of the family

again. If not, I would respond by taking away privileges, or giving them more time if I felt it would be fruitful.

- Our children always had to take responsibility for what they had done wrong. If they had wronged anyone, they would have to apologize and take full responsibility for their actions. They were never allowed to say something like "I'm sorry for my half of the argument." True repentance does not accuse others. As much as possible, they had to make things right with the other person. I remember one of my sons apologized to his friend, and then he followed up by even apologizing to his friend's father, that he might take full responsibility for his actions.

- If a spanking was in order, I made sure it was an occasion and not a swat with the hand. Time was needed for it to be effective. That meant I had to pull away from friends or activities I was involved in to do it correctly. I used a wooden spoon for spanking, never my hand. Hands are for affection, affirmation and love.

- Sometimes I gave correction by taking away privileges. And sometimes I gave added responsibilities.

- I did not correct the children in front of their friends. Embarrassment was not part of the deal. I even let them stay in their room for a few minutes following a spanking, so they would not be embarrassed in front of their siblings.

One of the most remarkable things would happen whenever I had to discipline my children. The child I had disciplined almost always came to sit on my lap following our time in his or her room. I never required it. But my children knew I loved them more than anything. The issue that brought about the discipline was never brought up again. Once they took ownership for a wrong and made things right, they were treated as though it had never happened. Our whole family was responsible to carry out the act of forgiveness to the corrected family member.

My Repentance

I remember on several occasions I had to repent to my family. If I was rude or impatient toward a family member, it was my turn to repent. Whenever this was needed, I mentioned specifically what I had done wrong. I remember one particular occasion when a driver pulled within inches of my car while I was driving on the streets of Santa Cruz, California. My parents lived there for many years, and we would take a week or two of our vacation time to stay with them every summer in what we called the Johnson Hilton. It was such fun for all of us.

This particular driver, however, had no concern for us whatsoever. If he had seen what he did wrong and somehow acknowledged that he had made a mistake, it would not have been a problem at all. But he did not. I became very angry at his disregard for the well-being of my family and our vehicle. I did not yell or say things I would later regret. But I was angry, and I let my horn do the talking. The bottom line was, my anger was very irresponsible. I remember turning to my family when the episode was over and confessing how wrong I was for my anger.

After I confessed, my son Eric said, "Yeah, Dad. You really blew it!"

He was right. He was not disrespectful when he said it. He was honest, which we greatly valued in our children.

Anytime I needed to repent to my family, I would then ask them to pray for me. They knew all I wanted to do was honor God, which I had failed to do in that moment. Their prayers for me were so sweet and forgiving as they laid their hands on their dad, who confessed to being wrong.

If I fail to lead by example in doing right, then I want to lead by example in repentance.

Insight from Proverbs on Discipline

The book of Proverbs is full of insight and wisdom on the topic of discipline. Here are a few proverbs on discipline that are too good to miss.

He who withholds his rod hates his son, but he who loves him disciplines him diligently.

Proverbs 13:24

Love always chooses the best. This is especially true with discipline, as love looks to the future and embraces the action that will benefit the child in the long run. Tenderness and humility are essential traits in carrying out discipline. Otherwise, we can be guilty of provoking a child to anger, which is forbidden (see Ephesians 6:4).

It is quite clear that God chastises us because of love. We, then, must do the same with great diligence. Foolishness is bound up in a child's heart, and it is the rod of discipline that brings deliverance:

Foolishness is bound up in the heart of a child; the rod of discipline will remove it far from him.

Proverbs 22:15

The rod unties what is bound. We all want our children to grow up with wisdom. But to ignore discipline because of inconvenience or the wisdom of the day is to make our children have to learn to deal with those issues later in life, when they are much more difficult to process.

In this passage, we find that discipline can rescue the soul of a child:

Do not hold back discipline from the child, although you strike him with the rod, he will not die. You shall strike him with the rod and rescue his soul from Sheol.

Proverbs 23:13–14

Once again, this discipline is not done in anger or vindication. That only fuels the foolishness of the child, creating hostility inside that can harden his or her tender heart. But if our discipline is done correctly, it can rescue the child from the hellish circumstances of life. It is worth it in the long run.

The rod of correction not only drives foolishness from a child; it also can give wisdom:

> The rod and reproof give wisdom, but a child who gets his own way brings shame to his mother. When the wicked increase, transgression increases; but the righteous will see their fall. Correct your son, and he will give you comfort; he will also delight your soul.
>
> Proverbs 29:15–17

A child who is brought up in the discipline of the Lord in a healthy manner will end up giving comfort to his or her parents, bringing great joy to their hearts. One of the great disasters in a home is seeing children have their own way. Such a cowardly approach to parenting breeds entitlement and absolute foolishness in them.

Tender Care

I love Proverbs 29:21, which describes the tender care we are to give our children: "He who pampers his slave from childhood will in the end find him to be a son." This kind of care is so powerful that it can even take a servant and turn him or her into a son or daughter. It really is remarkable, as the power of tender loving care transforms the identity of servants into sons.

"Therefore be imitators of God, as beloved children" (Ephesians 5:1). Children mimic their parents. Giving them a model to follow and copy is crucial. Being the example for them of how to live life is one of our greatest privileges. This does not mean we must be perfect. But even in our blemishes, they can learn from us. My friend Shawn Bolz says that God allows our closest friends to see our idiosyncrasies so they will always know that when God uses us, it is always by grace. If ever that truth applied to a specific context, it has got to be in the home. We teach by example the beauty of grace.

This next passage, written to the church at Thessalonica, uses the language of family to communicate its message. Paul wanted to reveal his affectionate and tender heart toward the believers there, using the language a mom or dad would use.

> But we proved to be gentle among you, as a nursing *mother tenderly cares for her own children*. Having so *fond an affection for you*, we were well-pleased to impart to you not only the gospel of God but also our own lives, because *you had become very dear to us*.
> For you recall, brethren, our labor and hardship, how working night and day so as not to be a burden to any of you, we proclaimed to you the gospel of God. You are witnesses, and so is God, *how devoutly and uprightly and blamelessly we behaved toward you believers*; just as you know how we were *exhorting and encouraging and imploring each one of you as a father would his own children*, so that you would walk in a manner worthy of the God who calls you into His own kingdom and glory.
>
> 1 Thessalonians 2:7–12, emphasis added

Paul used words like *tender care, fond affection, devout, upright and blameless*, and *exhorting and encouraging* to describe his value for these believers. But he borrows from the family setting to reveal his heart. These are the words that describe the privileged role of parents in caring for and serving their children.

Tender Children, Tender Treatment

In our home, Leah was always the one with an extremely tender heart. One time while I was traveling in ministry, Beni found her weeping. When she asked her why, Leah said it was because of how much I would miss her. Before I had left on my trip, I had let Leah know that I would miss her very much. Perhaps I overdid it! She cared so much for how I felt and thought. Values such as tenderheartedness and empathy go a long way in inspiring obedience before God and man.

Leah was the one whom I could usually discipline with my eyes. Literally. If I looked at her and her attitude was not what it should be, she would melt and fix it.

93

Each child is unique and should be treated accordingly. Wisdom is once again the most essential part of our toolkit. It helps us recognize the need and the process desired to bring about God's purposes.

Raising Adults

Remember, we are raising children to be adults and future parents. These are the adults who will matter most to us in the years to come. Having meaningful relationships with our children while they are young, and partnering with them for their future success, will make all the difference in the world as they grow into adulthood. This in itself makes a case for godly discipline.

Having adult children whom you respect, honor and celebrate is priceless. I celebrate Eric, Brian and Leah as my children. They bring me more joy than I could possibly have earned in a million lifetimes. But I also honor them for who they are. Who and what they have become moves me beyond words.

8

Trained to Know God

OUR CHILDREN GREW UP with the routine of attending corporate Sunday gatherings. Church was a place of social interaction, and they loved being with their friends. I am sure that helped make it something everyone looked forward to. But sometimes having them sit through a sermon or be involved in worship was a challenge. Of course, we worked to make the meetings beneficial to everyone. But usually, a child would rather be outside playing than have to sit through a meeting. The same could be said for many adults. If we don't have an appetite for what happens in those gatherings, attending is regarded as a chore—something to endure. "A sated man loathes honey, but to a famished man any bitter thing is sweet" (Proverbs 27:7). This verse means that people who are full don't even appreciate the luxuries of life. But those who are hungry (living aware of personal need) treasure the lesser things. This applies in the spiritual as well as the natural.

In the church we pastored in Weaverville, we decided to have our children join us for worship, and then we would release them to their special program, which they enjoyed. There were no special children's activities during our evening services. The children were with us the whole time. We chose to reward our children whenever they were involved in worship. There was no reward if they were not. In fact, there was a measure of correction, especially if they misbehaved. If they worshiped, we bought them an ice cream, which they of course loved. I know there are those who would criticize this kind of parenting, calling it *bribery*. We called it *reward*. The biblical concept we used came from Hebrews 11:6: "And without faith it is impossible to please Him, for he who comes to God must believe that He is and that He is a rewarder of those who seek Him."

Our misunderstanding of the subject of reward has weakened our understanding and practice of faith. Some foolishly say they are not interested in reward. But reward is a biblical concept that reveals the nature of God our Father. We must adjust to Him, not reduce Him to look like us.

Gather and Serve

The corporate gatherings were an important part of who we were as a family. Our children grew up knowing certain things were nonnegotiable. Joining the church family for corporate times of worship was one of those things. We discovered that the children benefited from what was happening, even when they were very young and seemingly not paying attention. Children pick up spiritual things quite easily, even when they are playing with toys or drawing. I feel sorry for children whose parents let them choose when to attend church. They miss out on the discipline of doing the right thing when it feels good and when it does not. And most of all, they lose out on exposure to the atmosphere that helps them construct an internal value system where the spirit man becomes trained.

Let us consider how to stimulate one another to love and good deeds,
not forsaking our own assembling together, as is the habit of some,

but encouraging one another; and all the more as you see the day drawing near.

Hebrews 10:24–25

We are supposed to think, intentionally, about specific things. Stimulating one another to serving God well in the corporate gathering is one of the expressions of this renewed mind. Not meeting together has become a habit for some, when God intended for us to develop a habit of meeting. Gathering together gives us the chance to bring encouragement to all. Some think freedom means disregarding all traditions and habits, and doing whatever feels right at the moment. Children raised in that environment are not ready to live in the real world and will most likely never kill their giants.

Children and the Holy Spirit

I heard an interesting story from a dear friend and seasoned saint, Iverna Tompkins. She mentioned that when the Spirit of God was moving powerfully in a meeting, they would instruct the parents to go get their children out of the nursery. Bringing children into that holy atmosphere has great impact on them. They learn His ways and learn to recognize His presence. This is one of the greatest gifts you can give your children—exposure to the glory of God.

"When Elizabeth heard Mary's greeting, the baby leaped in her womb; and Elizabeth was filled with the Holy Spirit" (Luke 1:41). Elizabeth was the mother of John the Baptist. Mary, of course, was the mother of Jesus. When both John and Jesus were still in their mothers' wombs, something extraordinary happened. Mary walked into the room and greeted Elizabeth. When she did, John leaped in Elizabeth's womb. Consider this: When the Son of God entered the room, even though still in His mother's womb, another baby recognized His presence and responded with joy. Elizabeth, too, was in turn filled with the Holy Spirit through the experience.

This story demonstrates a child's ability to recognize the Holy Spirit. Don't underestimate what children can discern, recognize and benefit from. Also keep in mind that some children have unusual sensitivities. Don't discount that or let it shock you. Pay attention when your kids have encounters with the Lord that are unusual, or when they have an experience level in the spiritual realm that you are not having. Ask questions, and help lead them into a place of real confidence in God through it. The Lord really honors their innocence and childlikeness. Value that unusual grace and gift on your children's lives.

The Boy Samuel

One of the principles I learned early in my parenting life comes from the story of the priest Eli and the boy Samuel. Hannah was a barren woman desperate to have a child. She prayed in such a deeply emotional way that Eli thought she was drunk. It was her despair he was seeing. In that kind of desperate position, it does not really matter to you what others think. When Eli recognized the genuineness of her prayer, he announced that she would have a son. Hannah named the child Samuel. She then gave her son back to God, taking him to live and serve with Eli in ministry:

> "For this boy I prayed, and the LORD has given me my petition which I asked of Him. So I have also dedicated him to the LORD; as long as he lives he is dedicated to the LORD." And he worshiped the LORD there.
>
> 1 Samuel 1:27–28

Hannah gave a gift somewhat similar to Abraham's, in that Samuel was the fulfillment of a promise from God to her, in the same way that Isaac was the fulfillment of a promise to Abraham. God rewarded her accordingly, and she bore three more sons.

Eli trained Samuel in the presence of the Lord, and the boy learned the priestly duties from an early age: "Now Samuel was ministering before the LORD, as a boy wearing a linen ephod" (1 Samuel 2:18). He was dressed in priestly garments, as the priesthood was to be his assignment in life. But the second time the Bible mentions that Samuel was ministering to the Lord, it says that hearing from God in any form was rare in those days: "Now the boy Samuel was ministering to the LORD before Eli. And word from the LORD was rare in those days, visions were infrequent" (1 Samuel 3:1). The backstory is that because of the rebellion of Eli's sons, the voice of the Lord was removed from those in ministry.

In that moment when hearing from God was rare, something happened. Samuel heard something. He ran into Eli's bedroom in the middle of the night because he thought Eli had called out to him. Eli told him to go back to bed. The same thing happened again, and Eli responded the same way. And then again. But after this happened for the third time, Eli realized that it might be God, and he gave Samuel instructions on what to say and do if God should speak again. God did speak, and a prophet was made. Samuel heard the voice of God and responded with a heart of surrender, manifested through obedience.

Here is the part of the story that really stirred my heart: Before God spoke that fourth time, the Bible says of Samuel, "Now Samuel did not yet know the LORD, nor had the word of the LORD yet been revealed to him" (1 Samuel 3:7). It suddenly became clear to me that Samuel ministered to the Lord but did not know Him yet. He did what he was supposed to do simply because it was right. We are to teach our children what it is to minister to the Lord and to serve Him wholeheartedly in the same way that Eli taught Samuel. Yet we must be aware that sometimes we are training children in the motions of something they don't yet understand. It was not until after God spoke to the boy Samuel a fourth time that a relationship was formed. Suddenly all the training, all the times in the presence with practical service and worship, made sense.

The principle is clear to me—we must teach children the ways of loving God, the ways of worship and the ways of personal devotion.

It is not training them in hypocrisy. Instead, it is creating a momentum that will make sense once they have their personal encounter with God. I personally think that this kind of training attracts the voice of God into their lives at an earlier age. It is what we do as parents; we set them up for their destiny in God.

Our oldest son, Eric, is now the senior pastor of Bethel Church. He recently preached a message to our church family in which he mentioned getting ice cream as a child for worshiping God. Of course, everyone laughed at the thought, but in a very supportive way. He then mentioned that one day it clicked, and he was worshiping God for real and not just for the ice cream. It is beautiful. We help create a momentum that God honors with an encounter. And those encounters change everything.

Raising Royalty

One of my favorite stories in the Bible is about Solomon. He was unqualified and unprepared to become the king of Israel, but at least he knew it. When God visited him in the night and offered him the chance to choose anything he wanted, Solomon knew enough to ask for wisdom (see 1 Kings 3:1–15; 2 Chronicles 1). This is a classic story, as those kinds of moments with God were the rarest of all gifts from Him.

The giant-killer himself raised Solomon. David, the *man after God's heart*, seemed to lack parenting skills with many of his children and suffered through horror stories with Absalom and his brothers. This problem still exists today. Some people are great at some things, but fail miserably at home. Thankfully, we are not required to sacrifice the family to become great at other things. We have to embrace the privilege of family with intentionality.

Something was different for David with Solomon, however. He raised Solomon with purpose and destiny in mind. Such vision can open us up for the wisdom we need for this task. Solomon described his training with David:

100

When I was a son to my father, tender and the only son in the sight of my mother, then he taught me and said to me, "Let your heart hold fast my words; keep my commandments and live; acquire wisdom! Acquire understanding! Do not forget nor turn away from the words of my mouth. Do not forsake her, and she will guard you; love her, and she will watch over you. The beginning of wisdom is: Acquire wisdom; and with all your acquiring, get understanding."

Proverbs 4:3–7

David planted seeds of hunger for wisdom in his son Solomon, who mentions his father's instruction to him in these verses. Solomon states that when he was a son to David, and the only son of his mother, who was Bathsheba, his father gave him those words of instruction. And that is exactly right. He was one of many sons to David, but was the only son of Bathsheba. Her only other child had been conceived in David's adultery with her, and that child had died right after birth.

In this fourth chapter of Proverbs, Solomon states that his father, David, taught him what was important in life. He taught him what his priorities should look like, and the price he should be willing to pay to obtain the priceless gift of wisdom from God. Wisdom is the great prize. And much like with the Kingdom of God, when this prize is sought for as a priority, all the other things in life are added as a blessing. It certainly worked this way for Solomon. Don't stumble over the fact that things did not end well for him. Wisdom only works when you use it. Solomon rejected his own teaching and counsel, but his successes are still worth studying. They are among the most amazing in all of Scripture.

As parents, we prepare our children with our instruction. Aggressively instructing them carries prophetic significance, because it prepares them to make choices they may not have had access to without our instruction. I wonder if perhaps Solomon is the only one who was given the *you can have whatever you want* option because he was the only one prepared to make such a choice. David trained him with his destiny in mind. We get our kids ready through prayer, teaching and encouragement, and then we have the privilege of watching God respond to their readiness with opportunities they might not have had otherwise.

Parents, we have the privilege of training our children for greatness. When we embrace the values we teach them, it goes a long way in enabling them to learn from us. When we live what we teach, we teach with authority, not just give out information. Our children can get information from a book, but they can only receive what a parent can impart to them when we as parents live it, teach it and prophesy it into our children's daily lives.

Cost and Reward

Pastors' kids are notorious for being troublemakers. Beni and I fought hard to protect our children from unnecessary pressures that could add their names to this statistic. Thankfully, our church family did not add unhealthy expectations that sometimes break a child, creating resentment and resistance to all things pertaining to church.

Even though we fought for them, our children still had to pay a price for who I was. And I could not control the price they had to pay. But what I could control was the reward they received for being my children. Some people call it nepotism. It really does not matter what others think or say. They are my children, and I must fight for their success and not sacrifice them on the altar of public opinion. I would gladly suffer for them where possible.

For this reason, I would look for opportunities to bless our kids because of my position. For example, if I spoke at a conference, I would bring Beni and the kids along so they could swim in the pool all day or go shopping. If we needed to hire someone to clean the offices, I gave one of my kids the chance to do it first. It is simple. But it is also powerful when you get to see what happens to children who grow up not resenting the Church, and instead celebrating it.

David Sought Reward

One of the more interesting stories in the Bible has to be the one concerning David and Goliath. What fascinates me about this story is David's response. We know that David ended up killing the giant, but it is how this scenario evolved that has me inspired and challenged.

David was a shepherd boy. His accomplishments were astonishing. He killed a lion and a bear when they tried to attack and steal the sheep. He killed them when no one was watching, so God could trust him to kill Goliath when everyone was watching. This is vital for understanding and celebrating our children's victories. They always lead to greater things, as that is the nature of God and His Kingdom—He only goes from glory to glory.

David's father asked him to bring some food to his brothers on the front lines of battle. When he did, he saw that Goliath was there, taunting the armies of God. This offended David, because he had a jealousy for the name of the Lord that one could only obtain in relationship. David was truly a worshiper who tended sheep for the glory of God.

David's oldest brother, Eliab, came on the scene and was angry to see David. It was a strange reaction to the presence of his younger brother. He accused him of irresponsibility and having wrong motives. (As I mentioned before, stay away from thinking you see the motives of another person. God alone knows the heart. If you can help your children learn that one, it will protect their hearts and minds from torment throughout their lifetime.) Eliab's reaction says more about him than it does about David. Like everyone else in the army, Eliab was terrified of Goliath. He needed someone to blame for his cowardice. David was the easiest target, especially when Eliab heard his little brother ask about the reward. It is important to remember that the hateful reactions from others toward us or our children speak volumes about those people, not about us.

David responded to Eliab's accusation by asking, "What have I done now? Was it not just a question?" (1 Samuel 17:29). And he went on to ask about the reward again: "Then he turned away from him to another and said the same thing; and the people answered the same thing as before" (verse 30).

Here is the part that has challenged my thinking from this story: David asked at least twice what the reward was for killing Goliath. And there is a good chance that he had also heard it for himself when it was first announced, since he was already there. Why is this so important? David was concerned with the reward. He heard what it was at least twice, and possibly three times. While he was provoked with jealousy for the name of the Lord, he was also mindful of God's economy, where people receive rewards.

Here is the reward that motivated David to pay attention to his convictions about the blasphemies uttered by Goliath: "And it will be that the king will enrich the man who kills him with great riches and will give him his daughter and make his father's house free in Israel" (1 Samuel 17:25). Personal gain has been labeled as evil, especially at a time when jealousy toward those who are blessed is at an all-time high. It is really sick that now jealousy is often labeled as a virtue—called, of course, by other names. It is called "fairness," "equality" and "human rights," to name a few. Such nonsense creates entitled believers who know little about paying a price for maturity. But God rewards such maturity. Gifts are free; maturity is expensive.

The Weakness of Fairness

We never allowed our children to say, "That's not fair!" We would respond, "Life isn't fair. You'll have to learn how to respond when things don't work the way you think they should." We wanted them to take responsibility for themselves, their actions and their reactions so they could make the most of the opportunities God alone could give them.

Jesus taught parables to help us understand how His Kingdom works. There is one story in particular that could enable us to see something that is so diametrically opposed to the spirit of the day that we owe it to ourselves to stop and take special notice. The parable is about a landowner who gives some talents to his servants (see Matthew 25:14–30). The talents were a sum of money that the servants were to invest for the landowner. One servant received five talents, another two, and another one.

There are only two parts of the story that I need to address. First of all, notice that not everyone received the same amount of money to invest. The landowner gave his servants resources according to their abilities. It is vital to notice that not everyone has the same abilities. This is the mercy of God. To give equal responsibilities to all would crush those who don't have the ability necessary for success.

The servants were then rewarded according to their measure of *faithfulness.* The second thing we must see is that faithfulness increases our ability. We see that in the way the landowner increased what the faithful servants had charge over. People are equal in value, but not in their gifts and responsibilities. Thankfully, there is no lid on the potential of someone who is faithful and brings increase for the King.

Probably the most offensive part of the story for some would be Jesus' response to the one who lived as a cowardly, unfaithful servant:

> But his master answered . . . "Therefore take away the talent from him, and give it to the one who has the ten talents." For to everyone who has, more shall be given, and he will have an abundance; but from the one who does not have, even what he does have shall be taken away.
>
> Matthew 25:26–29

This story ruins Jesus' chance at being politically correct. He is advocating taking money from the one who has the least and giving it to the one who has the most. If there is anything that angers those seeking equality, it is this.

Equality is important in that everyone gets a chance to succeed, and everyone has the chance for reward. This story shouts that there are no limitations to our potential increase. In reality, none of us can control where we start in life. But we do have great influence on where we end up, as reward is given to the faithful.

I treat my children with equal love, opportunities for success, and favor. This is my joy, as I do love them the same. But I also love them uniquely since they are so different from each other. At a time when children receive participation trophies for doing nothing but showing up, we need to make sure our children are not ignorant of how God works. I will always celebrate the efforts of my children, and now of my grandchildren, simply because they tried. I just don't want to make myself appear politically correct by hiding the fact that God does give rewards.

Teach your children to think. Political correctness is society's way of adding pressure for conformity. Political correctness is also proof that stupidity is contagious. Keep away from mob thinking, and embrace the ways of the Kingdom. God values the individual and the corporate identity. He will keep you and your household safe from the invaders who long to violate the values of His world that become ingrained in us.

To make this practical, it means that I have to be willing to give ice cream to my children who worship and to withhold it from any who don't. I do this knowing that next Sunday, there will probably be 100 percent participation. Teaching our children to understand and live in the essential principles of loving and serving God pays off in the long run. They inherit a momentum that gains interest through the years.

9

Prophetic Direction

ONE OF THE CORE VALUES of the Christian faith is that God still speaks. It would be impossible for us to be born again otherwise. God called us to Himself, and we responded with surrender.

In certain parts of the Church, the alarms go off whenever this subject is brought up. The concern is that if God speaks, then it could replace Scripture. That concern is legitimate in part, as some have wandered from the faith by adhering to any voice or impression they hear. We must never allow anything to violate or surpass the standard already given in Scripture. The Word of God is Jesus in print. He is the Word, so the Word must be treasured accordingly.

Building our lives, and especially our homes, on a subjective opinion (in conflict with Scripture) will not stand the test of time—especially for those who long to raise children who make a difference in the world. This must be a nonnegotiable issue. There is too much pressure on the home for us to have any hope of significant achievement without building the family on the Rock. And that Rock is Jesus Christ, the Word of God. All Kingdom accomplishments come from the life and strength of His Word.

Having said that, I affirm that God does still speak. This is the beauty of a relationship with God our Father. He longs to speak to His children. But His voice is not usually the thundering voice we see in the movies. He usually speaks as a friend.

The beauty of this journey is that He wants to talk to us about our lives, and especially about our children and grandchildren. He has all the insight we need to serve our children well. Learning to hear from God about a specific child or a specific need in the home can make the difference between abundant life and survival in the atmosphere of family life.

Nurtured and Known

We have a very deliberate process in working with our children at Bethel Church in Redding, California, that could be helpful to parents everywhere. We keep a file for each child by name. When children come into our care, regardless of their age we create a file for them. Those who work with the children are encouraged to pray and hear from God for that child. Sometimes they will get a glimpse of a strength God has given that little one, and sometimes they receive what we would call a prophetic word for that child. Please understand, never is a word given in our environment to control or influence a child's destiny in an unhealthy way. God will confirm what He has given us, or He will show that it was not from Him. The point is, we believe He speaks, we listen and we repeat what He says.

As the child advances from our nursery into the next class, the file goes with him or her. The teacher then takes notice of what has been spoken over that child, and also takes on the same responsibility to add to what has been spoken. The prophetic is supposed to encourage and edify each person into his or her God-given destiny. This is done for every child, in every class. When that young person graduates into our high school class, the file goes with him or her again. That way, our young people already have a history in God and in knowing what He says about them. This has become such a vital part of our training for children. The file of *what God says about them* follows them through their life.

I don't know that parents have to keep a prophetic file on each of their children, but I do think it is wise to stay mindful of what God says about each child. It becomes the fuel for prayer, and it is the confession we make both when things look good and when things look as if His will could never happen.

Zacharias prophesied over his son, John the Baptist, when the child was only eight days old (see Luke 1:67–79). I doubt the baby understood anything that was spoken. But the prophetic word just needed to be said. Some of the things we hear from God as parents and grandparents just need to be spoken. Nothing happens in the Kingdom until something is said. The prophetic word reveals the heart of God. And the heart of God must be declared!

The Fight for Identity

I remember one of the experiences I had while teaching a junior high Sunday school class. There were up to nineteen boys at a time in a room that measured about twelve by fourteen feet. A room that small is not the best environment to try to teach any group like that. But those boys, with their energy level, were a little bit crazy. They were constantly climbing the walls. In hindsight, I don't blame them.

One Sunday, I remembered the concept of how Jesus spoke to Peter, calling him a *rock* even though he lived like his given name— *broken reed*. So we were all in the classroom together, and I thought I would try something different. I sat down and said, just quietly, "You know, you guys are men of God."

As I began to talk to them about what I saw in their lives, you could hear a pin drop. They just all sat down and put their attention on me. I did not have to correct anyone. They were so hungry for anything that helped establish identity in them that they literally soaked in every word I had to share. Every word. They were in the fight for identity.

Prophetic Parents

It is easy to feel unqualified for certain challenges in life. And there are probably very few things for which the average parent feels less qualified than being prophetic. It might help us if we consider the issue from a different angle. Instead of attributing the prophetic to a gift that we have or don't have, consider this: In God's economy, certain graces (divine abilities) come with the position He gives us, not because of our personal gifts or talents. For example, even ungodly kings and leaders receive a gift from God that enables them to rule well. How they use that ability is up to them, of course. But the ability comes through the office or responsibility they are given.

This means that God has enabled parents to obtain a prophetic grace for the family simply because of their role as parents, and because they ask. This is really an important part of how God's world functions. Not only that, but we are commanded to "desire earnestly spiritual gifts, but especially that you may prophesy" (1 Corinthians 14:1). The point is, not only is it legal to pursue specific gifts (expressions) of the Holy Spirit; it is commanded. As parents, we need this in a big way. Prophetic seeing is essential for raising children.

Since the prophetic enables us to see, our perception of issues becomes clearer, as does our ability to see things like destiny, purpose, callings, etc. This is available for every believer, but especially to the parent for his or her family. We need every advantage that God has provided for us.

You may not be in a church that prays and prophesies over the destiny of your children. But you do serve the same heavenly Father, who has given you access to the same information. We have no excuse not to pursue God for our children, as we all have access to everything that God has provided for us to succeed as parents. We must utilize this advantage to hear from God specifically for our children.

In our case, Beni and I started praying for our children while they were still in the womb. At that time we even started praying for their future spouses, that God would bless and protect them.

The more you pray *Spirit-led prayers*, the more you pick up God's heart for your children and their future. I make the *Spirit-led prayer* distinction because there are some parents who pray their own wills in such an unbending way that they no longer can discern the will of God in a matter. We are to pray with boldness, but also with a surrendered hunger for His will. Praying yielded prayers opens us up to insight and prophetic perspective. Once we gain His perspective, bold prayers are the order of the day. Our confidence is in His will, His design.

For Beni and me, the prophetic sense of what God was doing in our children's lives evolved through the years. In other words, we did not always receive the insights we needed in a sudden experience. They unfolded as we pursued God and embraced the privilege of being involved in shaping our children's lives. Sometimes receiving insight felt like a supernatural experience, in that God put something in our hearts for which there seemed to be no reason. And yet most of the time, insight came not only from our prayerfulness, but also from our observation of our children's abilities and desires.

Prophetic Friends

Another beautiful advantage for us was that we had real prophet friends who loved our children. We had them come and minister at Mountain Chapel, where we pastored. We were also privileged to have them in our home. Their prophetic gift, exercised both in church and in our home, was of extreme importance to us (I talk a little more about this in a later chapter). But we treasured them even more as people. Their heart for God, and their character in and out of the pulpit, made it easy to receive from them. I cannot imagine where we would be without the investment they made in our lives.

While not everyone has the same access to seasoned prophets, everyone has access to a heart of hunger for the word of the Lord over their children. God has wonderful ways of getting His resources to His people, regardless of how well they are connected to the right people. Whether it is concerning money or a word from the Lord, or even open doors of favor, He will resource His people for His purposes.

Just be hungry to hear from God. Lift your voice to Him, asking for specific insights into your child's place in the world, and He will speak.

Jesus' Personal Key

Jesus told us He only did what He saw His Father do, and He only said what He heard His Father say (see John 5:19; 12:49). This is an important example to learn from, as Jesus did not live in reaction to the devil. He lived in response to the Father. This same principle will work wonders in leading our homes. The bottom line is, we learn *not* to live in reaction to problems, but to use those situations to respond to what the Father is doing. Responding to children instead of reacting to them is always more fruitful.

Jesus was sent to minister to the Jew first, to complete the requirement of the Old Testament. We know that was His commission from the Father. But there were times when He stepped outside this mandate. We know those times could not have been in violation of the principle of only doing the Father's will, so there must have been another factor involved that I think could help us immensely in raising our children. It is the faith factor. When a Syrophoenician woman came and asked Jesus to cast the demon out of her daughter, He said He could not give the children's bread to dogs. Healing and deliverance were the children's bread, He told her, first given to the children of Israel.

Yet that was not the end of the story for this mother. Her heart for her daughter was greater than her desire to take offense at His comment. (It amazes me how often our miracle is actually on the other side of getting through personal offense.) She answered Him that even little dogs eat the crumbs from the children's plates at their master's table.

112

When Jesus heard her response, He announced that the demon had left her daughter (see Mark 7:24–30). It is such a beautiful story. How did Jesus know that this was what the Father was doing? He did not seem to know it ahead of time. My opinion is that He knew what the Father was doing by seeing the faith in this mother's eyes. She could only get that gift from God, so that is how He knew what the Father was doing.

What an exquisite privilege we have as Christian parents to exercise the faith factor in responding to the issues at hand. Like this faith-filled woman, we can expect the Lord to move on behalf of our children.

Choosing a Direction

We have all heard the tragic stories of parents who live their lives of personal disappointment or failure through their children. In other words, they fight for their dreams for their own lives to be fulfilled in their children, because they missed fulfilling their dreams themselves.

There are also the cases where parents have been very successful in life and want the same for their children. That of course starts well, as I would hope that every parent would want their personal blessing to be passed on to their descendants. But the tragedy occurs whenever parents control or manipulate their children to get them to pursue the parents' dream for them, so the children become successful in the exact same way as their parents.

Either case is devastating, leading children to frustration and failure at best, and rebellion and forsaking the family at worst. God has a unique purpose for each child, and a healthy parent can help in the discovery of it.

All parents want the best for their children. It is part of being a mom or dad. We see people making dumb decisions in life and want so badly to keep our children from such decisions. Or perhaps we have seen our children make poor choices, and we want to protect them from those patterns of failure or disappointment. I find no fault with such desires. But it is vital that we return to the *owner's manual* to find out how to raise children correctly. The Bible has very specific instructions on how we are to raise our kids, and in what direction we are to lead them: "Train up a child *in the way he should go*, even when he is old he will not depart from it" (Proverbs 22:6, emphasis added).

Please notice that the verse says "in the way he should go." It does not say that we should train up a child in the way we want him or her to go. It does not say that parents know best. For example, if you are a medical doctor, don't force your children to become doctors. Pay attention to their own gifts and desires, and follow their lead in order to develop them as individuals. Athletes often have a hard time when their children have little athletic ability or interest. They will sometimes coerce a child into playing a sport that only frustrates him or her. Learn to recognize "the way he should go." Raise your children to love God, enjoy life and pursue their unfolding life's adventure with God.

The Impact of Worship

Both of my boys are very athletic. They have unusual gifts in playing a number of sports quite well. Baseball was our primary sport, though, since I also played it in high school with a decent measure of success. Eric played well enough for his high school team that he was given an MVP (most valuable player) award out of about seventy or eighty high schools in Northern California. He was a catcher. His batting average was over .580, and he never struck out all season. Brian was following in his footsteps. His skills in baseball were promising, like his older brother's. Although two years younger than Eric, he was already making his mark in sports, playing for the varsity baseball team as a freshman. He played basketball as well. His basketball shot was beautiful. They were both a great joy to watch, and we traveled all over the northern part of California to watch them play. When one of them would make a great play, I would stand up in the grandstands and yell, "Whose son is that?!"

One day, seemingly out of nowhere, Brian quit all sports. Just like that, almost overnight. This was a shock for us, as sports had been such a large part of the boys' lives growing up together. We had given ourselves in time, money and encouragement to our children's interests, regardless of what they were. The boys' passion was sports, and it seemed as though they had groomed themselves throughout their early childhood years for what they would accomplish in high school. But Brian lost all interest. Suddenly. Years of preparation seemingly were gone.

To say this was a concern is a great understatement. I was worried for him. We talked it through, and he was done with sports for a number of reasons. He picked up a guitar, something he had never shown interest in before, and he began to teach himself how to play. He played for hours a day. Sometimes on weekends he would play eight, ten or twelve hours a day. He had a friend in the church youth group who was equally as devoted to playing drums as Brian had become with the guitar. They played their music together for hours.

Music was always a large part of my life. My parents were very accomplished musicians. In some ways this should not have been such a shock with Brian, yet it was. While I was concerned, I also believed in my son. We walked through his change in interests, giving him our full support. But I also wondered in the back of my mind if it was not just a temporary fascination with something different, although Brian was not given to carelessness. Yet to do my part, I made sure he had a quality guitar and the best amplifier available for his needs.

Oftentimes, Brian would have a number of friends come over to the house to hang out. Night after night, this is what would happen: They would be having fun, and then without warning, I would notice that Brian would be gone. I would go to the back of the house, where his bedroom was, and I would hear him worshiping God with his guitar. He would then be out of sight for the rest of the night. Eventually, his friends would go home. Hours and hours of practice were his norm, with hours and hours of worship and writing songs almost daily, glorifying God.

After we moved to Redding to pastor Bethel Church, I remember times when Brian and his friends would go to a local park where there were various summer activities going on. But Satanists would also gather there in their own group. Brian would take his guitar and walk toward the Satanists' group while worshiping God. They would scatter quickly, as they could not handle the presence of God that was upon his music. Today, Brian leads our worship ministry at Bethel Church, as well as our Bethel Music label.

Starving for Encouragement

Educators tell us that it takes seven positive comments to recover from one negative comment. This is really astonishing. I remember my dad telling me about this concept showing up in his black Labrador as she cared for her many puppies. The dog would correct a puppy and bring it back into the fold, but then lick it seven times. It seems to be written into nature itself that everyone is in need of encouragement.

I remember one time that I had corrected Eric for several things as we were getting into our car to go somewhere. As I looked over to the church property, I noticed that he had left his bicycle there, which was a sure way of getting it stolen. As I began to point it out to him, Beni put her hand on my leg and said, "I think he's had enough."

She was right. There is a point where correction is more a release of our frustration than it is a help in serving and bringing direction to a child. That was the case in this moment, for sure.

Our role as parents is governmental, as I mentioned earlier. And that role is to protect and empower. But it is *encouragement* that is one of the primary ways we empower people to become all that God intended. That means we intentionally look for what they have done well and where they are trying and working hard. Calling attention to that works wonders. Think of the word *en*-courage. What we do for people instills courage in them. And this is an hour when everyone needs greater courage. The courage we need for life's hardest decisions can only be found as we make these decisions with eternity in mind.

My mom and dad were the greatest encouragement in my life. That was true even into my fifties, until my dad went home to be with the Lord. My mom is still a constant encouragement to me. As though I had just made a great play in baseball, even today she will sometimes yell out, "Whose son is that?!"

We worked hard always to encourage our children. A lot. Our boys were becoming young men, with real wisdom and devotion. Leah was growing up responsibly, too, but she was four years younger than Brian and six younger than Eric. We just did not know how she would respond to being pressured for her convictions when she got into high school. One day, Beni let Leah walk from Trinity County Christian School to Trinity High School, where her brothers attended. She was to meet them, hang out for a bit, and then Beni would pick them all up and take them home.

As Beni drove up to get them, she saw Leah in the face of a much older boy. Apparently, he had used foul language in front of her, and she had politely asked him to stop. He did not, so she got in his face and told him in no uncertain terms that he *must* stop. She was tenderhearted, but she was also unrelenting and determined for righteousness. She would even ask the driver of a car to change the music if she felt it was inappropriate.

Beni was relieved when she saw how Leah handled that situation at the high school, knowing our "little" girl would be just fine. It is wonderful to see that what you taught was actually caught.

Praying with Insight

As parents and grandparents, we are positioned to be part of the team that brings strength and courage to our young. This process begins with prayer for our children. It is given to us as parents to pray for their success in life, that they would become all that God intended. We are more likely to recognize the hand of God on a life when we are invested in that person's well-being through prayer.

It is important to realize that even within a given family, there are unique distinctions between siblings. Some children are very academic, while others are athletic, and still others are artistic. The point is, they each have God-given uniqueness that we need to value. Treating our children uniquely is a gift we owe them.

Pay attention to your children's gifts and interests. Children have unique talents that will ultimately influence what they become in life. Give them permission to have a passion about something. Get behind that passion and fuel it! You may not have unlimited resources to do that, but you have some. Draw from your friendships and other connections with people who have succeeded in areas your child is interested in.

Don't get upset, however, if your children's interests change from one season to another, as Brian's did. Like Thomas Edison inventing the lightbulb, they need the exposure to what does and does not work for them. They are gaining experience. You don't want to trim or control their passion, or change it. Just watch for it; it is there as God's gift.

It is about calling out the gold in people. Perhaps you have heard the statement "If you do what you love, you'll never work a day in your life." Doing what we were born for is rewarding and exhilarating. It also has powerful impact on the world around us, because we become something according to God's design. And in doing so, we have found how to live our life in joy.

The famous artist Pablo Picasso had a mother who believed that her child would become something significant. As the story goes, he told someone, "My mother said to me, 'If you are a soldier, you will become a general. If you are a monk, you will become the Pope.' Instead, I was a painter, and became Picasso." He found his passion and had an impact on the world through his gift. Anyone who discovers who God made him or her to be will never want to be anyone else.

The second part of Proverbs 22:6 is as important as the first part: "Even when he is old he will not depart from it." This is a wonderful promise that sometimes takes a while to see come to fruition. I read an amazing story some time ago about a section of land in the middle of a desert that researchers wanted to experiment with. There was water underground, so they decided to water this section without planting any plants or even seeds. They just added water to the desert. What happened next is simply amazing. A great variety of plants grew, forming a jungle-like atmosphere. All the researchers had done was add water.

Our job is to plant the seeds in our children's lives, and then cover their lives with prayer. Prayer brings the water, so to speak. And it is God who will bring forth fruit from the seeds we have planted.

The point is, we are always responsible to plant in hope, knowing that God is able to make up for our lack of parenting skills. Our children become giant-killers purely by grace. And that grace is activated through the power of God's Word over their lives. We have a role. Just do it.

10

Praying from the Unseen

O UR SPIRITUAL MATURITY is never any greater than our relationship with the Holy Spirit. He is central to all things
pertaining to becoming Christlike. One of the greatest tools
of the believer is the ability to recognize the Spirit of God at work in
any given situation. A partnership develops from the awareness of
the One who by nature will only lead us into health and strength in
our families. By the way, Jesus is called the *Eternal Father* in Scripture (see Isaiah 9:6), which gives us a glimpse into Jesus' ability to
seamlessly represent the Father in all things. And the *Eternal Father*
really knows how to do family.

Having said that, I want to add that anointed prayers are very similar to authentic prophetic words. Both come from the Holy Spirit,
have their roots in the Word of God and reveal His heart for the immediate moment. It is important to learn to recognize prayers that
attract the Holy Spirit.

We have the privilege and responsibility to pray over our children.
Praying prayers that the Holy Spirit says *amen* to is one of the greatest joys ever. In doing so, we become involved in bringing the heart,
as well as the hand, of God to our families. Learning to recognize

the Holy Spirit's response to what you pray helps bring exponential increase to the effectiveness of your prayers. I recognize His response often through an increased awareness of His presence, which is usually manifested through a dramatic increase of peace. And then, sometimes, I am able to recognize *His amen* by what I call *inspired thoughts.* This is usually where He takes me deeper into a prayer direction with greater insight than I would have had normally. It basically means that I just had an idea that is better than one I could have come up with myself. I often end up praying something that I had no knowledge of until that moment—praying from the unseen. For me, this is another sign that I am praying anointed prayers.

If you will keep prayer a two-way conversation, you will discover the beauty of prayers inspired by the Holy Spirit. By learning to recognize Him in your prayers, you will be entrusted with the honor of revealing His heart at a whole new level. Whenever we discover that great treasure, we see where we can co-labor with the Lord to see His purposes in our family line. This kind of praying takes time, insight and persistence. He is moved by this in a profound way and adds the weightiness of His presence to it all.

The Work of Prayer

Praying prophetic words over our children is much like working yeast into a lump of dough. It requires effort and time. This means we must take what God has said over their lives and pray it into them with unrelenting force.

I realize that this may sound contradictory to some who are thinking, *If God said it, surely it will happen without our prayers.* This is true in some cases. But oftentimes, God speaks to us about the issues of life and gives us a promise that requires our participation. Abraham received the promise of a son. But he still had his part to play in its fulfillment, since his son Isaac was not immaculately conceived. Some of God's promises are announcements of potential, which He is not obligated to fulfill. They become effective when we do our part. Prayer followed by obedience is a beautiful expression of our partnership with God.

I work very hard to meditate prayerfully on what God says about me. I have learned everything else is a lie. In fact, I try never to entertain a thought in my head about me that is not in His head about me. Life is hard enough without my helping the devil discourage or distract me. What God is saying will protect the identity and faith of any serious disciple of Jesus.

I take a promise from God about any area of life and pray it, confess it quietly, declare it loudly and sing it. I sometimes type it on a page in my iPad or put it on 3x5 cards to carry with me. The point is, I surround myself with what God is saying, and then I surround my walk with God with those same promises turned into prayers, confessions and songs. It is my responsibility to be a watchman over my household, which means I keep my ears and eyes open to any challenge we face and the promise He has already put in place to enable us to overcome it in great victory.

Whenever we are good stewards of anything God gives us, He adds more to what we already have. Faithfulness attracts more. That is a Kingdom principle that works with money, friends, favor, and now with insights for prayer. If we use what little we have in order that His purposes might be developed in the lives of our children and grandchildren, He will open our eyes to see more of what needs to happen and how. He generously gives to those who steward His Kingdom well.

Learning from Job

Job was a heroic figure in the Old Testament, renowned for his courage and faithfulness to God, regardless of his circumstances. His wife told him he should curse God and die. So even his support system, which probably functioned well while he was blessed, turned against him in trial. Much is revealed in the challenge of our faith.

Job had a prayer focus concerning his children that I have found useful:

> His sons used to go and hold a feast in the house of each one on his day, and they would send and invite their three sisters to eat and drink with them. When the days of feasting had completed their cycle, Job would send and consecrate them, rising up early in the morning and offering burnt offerings according to the number of them all; for Job said, "Perhaps my sons have sinned and cursed God in their hearts." Thus Job did continually.
>
> Job 1:4–5

This is a remarkable way to intercede for our children. Every parent alive should learn the timing of Job's prayers, as they were not connected to a record or report of sin. He simply wanted to make sure his children were covered, in case in their celebration they became careless and sinned against God.

Many people who can trust God in trial fall apart in blessing. Job knew this and made sure to cover his sons and daughters during their feasting. His children were most likely adults by this time, but he still felt the need to cover them with prayerful intercession. This is the beauty of parenting.

Persistency and Consistency

Beni and I prayed with our children nightly before putting them to bed. This was not just a cute activity we did only when they were small. It continued into their teenage years. We did it every night, unless I was out of town or got home late from a meeting. And if I got home after the kids were already in bed, I would go pray over them while they slept. That part was a habit of mine even if we had prayed together before they went to sleep. I prayed the promises of God over them. Sometimes I would simply declare those promises. I did these things very quietly, so as not to wake them, but in my heart

I was shouting what God had said over their lives. Then there came a time when they started going to bed later than I did, so occasionally I got up in the night or early in the morning and prayed over them. The point is, prayer over family members and their destinies becomes the most powerful parenting tool, especially when it is followed by our obedience.

I also loved to challenge my kids in their faith and understanding. Random comments helped, although I had to be careful not to make my comments into sermons. There were a couple of things I said to the kids repeatedly, night after night. One was, "Before you go to sleep tonight, ask God if there is anything that's impossible that He wants you to do." Sometimes I would simply make a statement over them, such as, "Remember, you are part of a team that is here to change the world." The point is, I wanted to connect them to their eternal purpose, over and over again. Becoming a giant-killer does not happen by accident. Killing the giants of impossibilities happens when we see that the heart of God is for us.

I never quizzed my children to measure the impact these things were having. That might have pressured them to perform for me. I was mostly interested in shaping their thought life. These were seeds that needed to sit for a while before germinating. Besides, some things I declared just needed to be said. It was vital to *work that word over their lives down into their spirits* through prayer and proclamation.

At this point, it could be very easy for you to picture these moments I had with my kids as powerful supernatural moments. And while that happened on occasion, most of the time it was the discipline of consistency. What was burning in my heart for them needed an outlet—and so I spoke.

When the yeast is in the dough, you can rest and watch the effect. The bread will rise. The Kingdom of God, that manifestation of God's dominion, is likened to leaven (see Matthew 13:33). Leaven is the yeast that will always affect its surroundings. One of the most wonderful things about leaven is that once it is worked into the dough, it can never be removed. It will have effect when it is exposed to heat. Our passionate prayers add the fire that causes the leaven of His promises to be activated in our children, causing the bread of their hearts to rise to its potential.

Good Words, Bad Words

I love hearing what God says about any subject, but especially about my children, my family and my friends. As a discipline, I review the words and promises God has given us over and over again. But not everything that is said is from God. There are careless people around us who will proclaim the poison of their own hearts into our children's lives. Some words are obviously damning. Others are innocent mistakes spoken by well-meaning people. Our job is to watch and pray.

People, even friends, will sometimes say things about your children that you just need to reject. Beni and I call it *flushing*, just like with our toilets. The similarity should become obvious. Don't ever feel as though you have to receive it when other people project their failures or struggles in parenting onto you. Neither are you obligated to receive their frustrations or challenges in parenting as things that will automatically happen to you. Reject those kinds of words. Flush those words immediately.

One time, a person called one of my kids a brat. I told the person that my child's behavior was wrong, but that being a brat was not my child's identity. I will not allow that kind of behavior from an adult toward a child.

These well-meaning but sometimes destructive comments people make begin right after a child is born. For example, few things are more perfect in life than a newborn baby. Most people are rightly attracted to that little one. But sometimes they follow up with careless comments about how all the baby does is cry, eat, sleep and make messes in his or her diapers. Most of the time it is an attempt at humor or being lighthearted, which really is not a problem. But sometimes humor hides pain and frustration.

Don't become immune to the subtlety of such words. Performance-oriented people are prone to speaking in such ways, since our little ones cannot yet do any tricks or act in ways that please people. Not at all. They are simply alive. They are living beings made in the image of God, and they can do nothing to earn love. We love them for being. And while careless comments seem harmless, they can take away the joy of caring for a little one who can do nothing in return.

These can be fragile moments, when you consider that most moms and dads are sleep-deprived for a while following the birth of a child. Listening to other people's complaints makes us more receptive to a distorted perspective. Remember, there are parents who have lost a child, and they would give anything to miss a night's sleep and to have the privilege of changing diapers again. Anything.

Love is unselfish. Caring for someone who cannot give in return is one of the most Christlike activities we can know in this life. This is the purest expression of love. Don't let anyone rob you of this great privilege through his or her carelessness.

And then someone comes along who talks about how cute the baby is now, *"But just wait until your child turns two!"* It can be terrifying to hear this, especially if this is your first child. Children around the age of two learn the word *No.* They begin to develop in ways that can be unnerving for any parent, let alone a first-time parent. God has answers to these seasons and challenges. Fearing such challenges exaggerates them.

Some people will then continue with, *"Just wait until they enter kindergarten and like getting away from home!"* Or they warn, *"Wait until your child turns ten and wants more independence!"* It seems that because every age has its own challenges, there are those who want to give you their negative perspectives.

Probably the most often repeated words of death are, *"Just wait until they become teenagers! You'll wish you'd never had children!"* Again, I am sure that many who talk like this are trying to be funny. In some cases, they are trying earnestly to prepare other parents for the challenges that are sure to come. Yet such words only hurt and never help.

We have friends who would give anything to have the messy room, or the broken window because a child accidentally threw a baseball in the direction of the house. They would give anything to have to wash their kids' clothes and cook for them again. They cannot, because of a tragic accident. Again, perspective produces hope and thankfulness.

Whenever people spoke these careless comments about children around us, Beni and I would look at each other, or even talk later, following the conversation, and we would intentionally reject what was spoken. We would *flush* their words. But we also followed this decision with a confession of what we were expecting in our household. We would get together and say something to this effect: "No, our children will not grow up to be disrespectful and destructive. They will not rebel and turn away from God. Our children's teenage years will be a joy for us all, as we discover who You made them to be, Lord."

God knows only forward motion, going from glory to glory. And everything He is in charge of continually moves forward. This is important, since it is the nature of God Himself that sets the parameters for the nature of family life to be discovered. Practically speaking, Beni and I expected each age and season of our children's lives to be better than the previous ones. From glory to glory. And honestly, that is how it happened. We loved and enjoyed each age the children went through. And we still do now, into their adulthood.

We determined early in life to find the gold that God had put into each season of our children's lives and call it out with promises, confessions and decrees. Our refusal to listen to negative words about them or about specific ages was very beneficial. We always rejected the thought that another parent's struggles or failures would automatically become our own. Such an approach was simple, but profound in its effect on our overall approach to our family life.

Don't Be Ignorant

It would be absolute foolishness and ignorance to pretend that there are no problems with raising children. Having a two-year-old helps us find out how materialistic we are. They tend to break things. Because of this, my uncle used to say, "Every household needs a two-year-old in it."

The early years of childhood do present challenges for us, as little ones have a God-given bent to find the boundaries of their own independence. The teenage years present a big list of prayer targets, as teens' bodies are changing, sexual appetites are forming, their relationships with their peers are becoming increasingly more important and their bent toward independent thinking is taking on new expression. The bigger the challenge, the bigger the victory. The bigger the giant, the bigger the reward. This is important, since our approach to these issues of life often determines the outcome.

I cringe whenever I hear a parent say how much he or she hates the teenage years, especially when a teenager is present. That emotionally separates these teens from the adults who should adore and admire them, and it places them only with their peers, who are usually clueless. They then see their peers as the only ones who understand them.

Our careless words create an impossible situation for our young people when we hate the season of life they are in, especially when you realize that it is impossible to change it. Think about it from their perspective—someone extremely important in your life hates the age you are right now, yet there is nothing you can do to change it. You cannot add years to yourself. Add to that the roller-coaster emotions that go hand in hand with the biological changes teens are experiencing, and you have a generation looking to all the wrong places to belong. Belonging is the quest of every person on one level or another. Remember, teenagers' bodies are developing at a rate that God designed, which means He has solutions and ideas to help make their teenage years glorious and victorious, in spite of the ups and downs.

Our challenges in raising children seem to get more and more intense and complicated as they grow older. Acknowledging the challenges is a good beginning place, if it helps us turn to the Lord in our need. Our approach must be with absolute trust in God, and we must have a healthy outlook filled with excited anticipation.

For many people, breakthrough begins the moment they stop being impressed with the size of their problem. If I feel overwhelmed by the evil in this world, I must turn my heart toward God until I become even more overwhelmed by His goodness. If I feel dumbfounded by my ignorance about how to face a particular problem, I must become increasingly aware that God has already gone ahead of me and has a very specific solution that I can come to know. If I become overly aware of my weakness in hearing His voice, I must put my affection on the One who knows how to speak loudly enough to be heard. The point is, none of us is at our best when we are more aware of our problems or inabilities than we are of the solutions we carry through divine assignment.

Bring Perspective

I remember Eric came to me once to tell me how much he hated English in school. He was somewhere around ten or twelve years old. I listened with interest. When he was finished, I did not correct him or tell him he was wrong for feeling like that. I understood frustrations with school out of my own experience. But I did tell him that he might want to pay special attention to that subject in school because he just might be one of those whom God would use to write books for His people. It was not a prophecy. It was an unassuming word I spoke to add perspective. Divine perspectives always bring hope.

Eric got a faraway look in his eyes at hearing that, a look he would get whenever he was pondering something. After a moment of thought, he said, "Okay, Dad." And that was the last of that issue.

I am not saying Eric loved English after that moment. But he was able to see purpose in the pain. He has since written two books and has many more books in him that will be brought forth in the years to come.

We have the privilege of speaking the promises of God in many different ways. Sometimes it is by quoting a Scripture. And sometimes it is by declaring a principle over our children's lives, as I did with Eric in the story I just mentioned. The point is, our words and actions *seed the clouds* of destiny over our families. If we don't have the prevailing word over our children, other people will. And the outcome probably will not be what God intended. Capture your moments, and capture His thoughts. Then make His thoughts known through decree, backed up with prayer.

Praying Scriptures

One of the best things we can do for our children is to pray what is written in Scripture over their lives. As I mentioned, I would pray over my kids while they were sleeping. I also quoted Scriptures over them when I prayed. Certain passages would stand out as important promises from God for our family, and they needed the attention given to them that can only come from prayer.

Our dear friends Wesley and Stacey Campbell have written extensively on this subject in their books titled *Praying the Bible* (Chosen, 2016, 2018). The Campbells really lead the way in this beautiful subject, having learned to merge the beauty of Scripture with the passion and power of prayer.

One of the directions that I have had in prayer for my children since their childhood, and now for my grandchildren, is that they would have a heart to know God. I prayed that specific prayer for a long time, and I got so excited when I saw that I was praying what was already in print on the pages of my Bible. Jeremiah 24:7

(emphasis added) says, "*I will give them a heart to know Me*, for I am the LORD; and they will be My people, and I will be their God, for they will return to Me with their whole heart."

It may sound strange that I was so excited when I saw this verse in the Bible. It should be an obvious prayer for parents to pray that would delight God's heart. But when I saw that it was a biblical prayer, it added such confidence for me, in that I was praying the heart of God. I could see on the pages of my Bible that He was already saying *amen* to what I had been praying.

Here is another biblical prayer that I prayed over our children: "Let our sons in their youth be as grown-up plants, and our daughters as corner pillars fashioned as for a palace" (Psalm 144:12).

Praying His Heart, His Word

My mother gave me (and all the parents in our family) a particular list of Bible verses that she has prayed faithfully for decades over her children, grandchildren and now great-grandchildren. I have used this list to pray these same Scriptures over our family members, and I am including them for you as appendix 4 at the end of this book so you can pray them, too. A beautiful rainbow of hope and protection is created over our children when we combine the beauty of Scripture with the privilege of prayer.

Children who are treasured as a gift from God and are celebrated as a reward from Him become powerful weapons of war:

> Behold, *children* are *a gift of the* LORD, the fruit of the womb is *a reward*. Like arrows in the hand of a warrior, so are the children of one's youth. How blessed is the man whose quiver is full of them; they will not be ashamed when *they speak with their enemies in the gate.*
>
> Psalm 127:3–5, emphasis added

As we have already seen, we were born into a war. And when children are raised in the atmosphere of being valued and celebrated, they grow into their eternal destiny with confidence as they go into their places of influence and confront the powers of darkness. Confidence in warfare, knowing you are treasured and celebrated, and a life without shame are all fruits of being raised in God's household.

I love to pray over my children and grandchildren regarding their nights. This passage from Isaiah describes how we are to awaken every morning, and how our children are to awaken—with the ear of a disciple/learner who is ready to say *yes* to God:

> The Lord GOD has given Me the tongue of disciples, that I may know how to sustain the weary one with a word. He awakens Me morning by morning, He awakens My ear to listen as a disciple.
>
> Isaiah 50:4

This is a beautiful description of what it looks like to have the Holy Spirit minister to you throughout the night, and then to awaken with the *yes* of a follower of Jesus already in your mouth. Covering our children in prayer with this purpose is a beautiful privilege.

Here is another Scripture that has been a very important passage for my family and me: "All your sons will be taught of the LORD; and the well-being of your sons will be great" (Isaiah 54:13). While this verse says "sons," the implication is for our children, as the New King James Version states: "All your children shall be taught by the LORD, and great shall be the peace of your children." Praying for our children to be taught of the Lord is vital. This quickly became one of the premiere verses for me to pray over my children.

The Ultimate Assignment

Praying these types of prayers for our children and grandchildren is one of the greatest privileges in life. We become tools in the hand of the Lord that shape the character and the destiny of their lives. But the ultimate task is to take this one step further. We must teach them to fight with their own promise. Paul spoke to his spiritual son,

Timothy, this way: "This command I entrust to you, Timothy, my son, in accordance with the prophecies previously made concerning you, that by them you fight the good fight, keeping faith and a good conscience" (1 Timothy 1:18–19).

What is the point? The promise of God is the weapon that must be used to bring our children into God's intended future. This must become one of the tools they use for themselves so that they come into all He intends. Larry Randolph, a gifted prophet and friend, once told us, "God will fulfill all of His promises. But Ie is not obligated to fulfill our potential." Much of what we ache for in life lies in the realm of our potential, for which God has given us promise. It is time to fight with His Word and teach our children to do the same.

The Word of God is a wonderful gift from Him. Many generations and even present-day cultures have been without the Bible. It has been the target of many wars and conflicts, with leaders of culture pronouncing its demise. And yet here it stands as the high standard for life, having been breathed by God Himself. It is our privilege to read it over and over again. I will not miss a day in the Word. What is more important is that this Word gets in me. I memorize it, quote it and sing it. But there is a great treasure yet to unfold for many. Learn to pray the Bible. It accurately reveals His will, His heart and His promise for you and your family. Praying the Bible is a necessary part of praying from the unseen.

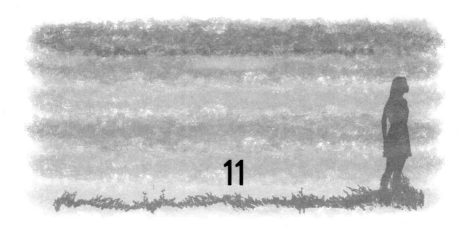

Government and Such

THE DEVIL LOVES to have influence in the home. If he wins there, he wins everywhere. And while I seldom talk about the powers of darkness, it is foolish to think that the vile one will lie down and ignore our efforts to raise up a generation with righteous influence in the earth. One of the primary tools he uses in this hour is government, for those who work in that world have God-given authority. Obviously, the devil uses media and education a lot as well. But those realms only have the authority we give them with our time and affection. Government has authority from God. And if the Bible has no influence on shaping the values and policy administrators set forth, those governments may be well-intended, but they will always go beyond the realm of responsibility God intended them to have.

It is the goal of the powers of darkness to have leaders in these governments overstep their role and make the individual family powerless. We need unusual wisdom to see the situation clearly and to know how to respond. Change is needed on all fronts. And much of it will come from the courageous ones we raise in our homes.

We live in a time when the influence of government in the home is on the rise. Some of it is a reaction to the horror stories caused by bad parenting. But there is a huge problem with this situation— God has not given the government the authority to raise children. Thus, its representatives lack the tools to be effective in what they are trying to do. They can protect. They can empower. But they cannot parent.

Usurping the role of the parent is a serious overstep often taken by leaders who are trying to build a utopian society through implementing their ideals. This is a laughable goal, as it always seems to be without Christ at the center. He is the cornerstone of all life and reason. Leaving Him out of the picture is the ultimate expression of arrogance and futility. We must return to the Designer's design by knowing Him, and relearn what government is to look like when it governs a healthy home.

God designed parents to carry authority over their families. Government has the right and responsibility to step in if there is criminal activity or a threat to the well-being of the children or a spouse. This must happen. Thanks to increased efforts to shut down sex trafficking, an evil that has affected nearly every nation, the government has focused more attention on protecting the vulnerable. This is a great improvement over previous generations. Yet the problem of *who gets to raise a child* remains. The government cannot parent a child. Period.

When Silence Screams

Either we teach our children intentionally about God, about life, about values, about individual responsibility and God's purpose and destiny for us, or our silence will teach them. Being unintentional in these things teaches them complacency, indifference, a divided heart, cowardly living and living for the temporal over the eternal. It is vital that we rise up and teach our children. We are the ones God has gifted to accomplish the impossible through the generation put into our charge. Like all gifts, teaching is best developed through consistent use.

Oftentimes, parents remain silent while the government takes their God-given responsibilities away. Such silence screams. Many in power would love nothing more than to control your home, branding your child with their naïve influence. They cannot give your child an aspirin at school without your approval, but in many states, they can allow your child to be given birth control or have an abortion without your approval. This is insanity. Absolute insanity. People who think like this have no right to rule.

Many government officials are well-intentioned, and they must react to the few people who exhibit great negligence in parenting. But good intentions cannot replace the wisdom of God's design. We must not give up our ground on this matter. Understanding the design of the Designer is critical. Prayerfully consider how to respond to the challenge you face in your part of the world.

Big government is needed where there is much sin. "By the transgression of a land many are its princes" (Proverbs 28:2). That is the nature of things in society. As sin increases, government grows to take care of the problem, when, in fact, the root is the breakdown of the home. Believe it or not, the answer to fixing most of the ills of society is healthy family life. It is scary to see what percentage of men on death row never had a dad. It is not complicated. The tide must turn through our diligent, and sometimes militant (in prayer and in the ballot box), approach to regaining influence in our states and nations. Giving ourselves to this noble task not only benefits our families; it contributes to the momentum for a generation to be restored to God's intent, while government returns to the roles that God gave it—to protect and empower. Can you imagine if our governmental leaders embraced those two roles wholeheartedly? Can you imagine what might happen to the following generations? The possibilities really are glorious and mind-boggling, if government leaders would honor God by applying themselves to their God-given assignment instead of violating His design through their arrogant fight for power.

How to Approach Educators

Zealously living the reality of God's design for the home will bring most of the other broken issues of society into a healthy place. Few areas of need around the world—whether the issue is poverty, immorality, racial tensions or military conflict—would not be healed through healthy families.

Today, society has created educational systems to help in the privilege of teaching children. We are blessed with skilled and compassionate people whose sole desire is to influence a generation of children into their purpose and destiny. This has been one of the gifts civilization has brought to its people. Initially, schools taught traditions, skills and religious values. But eventually, schools were created to teach more specific areas of knowledge like math, reading and writing. I don't disagree with this process, as long as it does not undermine the role of the parent. Yet tragically, undermining the role of the parent has become the spirit of the day. We should be able to have the best of both worlds in professional teachers who are delegated by the parents, not the government, to train our children. We must be involved in our children's education to ensure our intended outcome.

We become "scary parent" followers of Jesus when we have the need to control our educators or educational system. We believers are sometimes known for what we want to control instead of where we want to serve. Educators automatically resist anyone trying to control them. They have a God-given gift of discernment that they must use to protect their responsibility to society not to be controlled by any group.

When there are concerns we ought to take action about, however, there is a way to approach educators and get results. We have found that showing love through the heart of a servant goes a long way in affecting our educational environment. When we serve educators and give them honor, we are much better positioned to voice our concern when there is an issue. Earn emotional currency toward that end by investing in those who serve your children and demanding nothing in return.

This Is War!

As I stated earlier, we were born into a war. I so hope this is clear to you. Otherwise, you will always be trying to make sense of the senseless, and you will find someone to blame for the unexplainable. We are at war. And lest I heighten your animosity toward the ungodly systems that surround us, let me remind you of the real battle. It is in the mind. It is for the mind.

We are not at war with people—not even those who want to take our children and raise them in antichrist environments. We are at war with the demonic powers that inspire and control those types of people. Prayer is our tool for victory.

The apostle Paul gives us priceless insight into this battle in 2 Corinthians 10:3–5:

> For though we walk in the flesh, we do not war according to the flesh, for the weapons of our warfare are not of the flesh, but divinely powerful for the destruction of fortresses. We are destroying speculations and every lofty thing raised up against the knowledge of God, and we are taking every thought captive to the obedience of Christ.

Fortresses are hiding places for the demonic. And those fortresses are described as speculations and lofty thoughts raised up against the knowledge of God. Putting it simply, these hiding places are realms of thought. At least in part, the demonic realm is concealed in the ideas and thoughts that are raised up in arrogant opposition to the knowledge of God. Taking our thoughts captive to the obedience of Christ is how we fight the battle against these spiritual minions. Our place of obedience here enables us to be effective beyond our own thought life. Once we have taken our thoughts captive, we illustrate a sanctified mind, evidenced by the attitudes outlined in

Philippians 4:8, "Whatever is true, whatever is honorable, whatever is right, whatever is pure, whatever is lovely, whatever is of good repute, if there is any excellence and if anything worthy of praise, dwell on these things." With a sanctified mind, we are positioned to take down the ideas that have been raised up against God through other people.

In a mostly negative sense, our media controls the narrative on any given subject. This is not just an American issue. It is world-wide. Living in the midst of a bombardment of demonic ideals is a challenging task, to say the least. One must be armed with truth.

But please note that to be truly effective, we must join truth with compassion. Consider our wonderful privilege of affecting how people see reality. We do not accomplish it through manipulation or control. We do it by removing the influence of the liar through prayer, praise and loving people in truth. People live in deception because they live under the influence of the liar. When we pray and take false ideologies captive to the obedience of Christ, we free people to see clearly, sometimes for the first time in their lives. This is the privilege we have.

For me, it looks something like this scenario: Let's say I have a neighbor who has committed a sin he feels is unforgivable, so he will not respond to the Gospel because he feels there is no use. My prayer for him goes something like this: *I take captive the thought that says God will not and cannot forgive my neighbor's sin. I declare in Jesus' name a revelation of the love of God, seen through His wonderful forgiveness, over his life. God's desire to forgive is far greater than this man's sin.*

By praying for him in this way, I deal with the realms of deception that have kept him in darkness. Obviously, this way of praying is vital over our children as well. This is especially important if you have a "prodigal" son or daughter. This way of praying is also useful for training our children in a divine strategy that keeps them anchored in love, while they avoid becoming embittered against people who hold to such destructive views.

The Problem with Truth

We know that the truth sets free. Freedom is one of the prevailing attributes of a citizen of the Kingdom of God. But it is common in Church history to see people who used truth to separate and abuse someone who thought differently. This kind of abuse is not a good thing for us to be known for, yet sadly, it has been the reputation of the Church for quite a while now.

Two of my heroes of the faith are John Wesley and George White-field. Both were great leaders in revival, shaping the course of history through their boldness, faith and powerful preaching of the Gospel. But they were at opposite ends of the theological ideal of the day. Charles Wesley, John's brother, sent a poem to Whitfield. In it were these words: "And must we, now in Christ, with shame confess, Our Love was greater, when our Light was less?"* In effect, we had more love when we had less light.

That is a stunning statement acknowledging that light (seeing truth) requires greater amounts of love if we are to remain in the center of Jesus' heart for this world. My dear friend and spiritual father Jack Taylor puts it this way: "We've murdered love with truth!"

Raising children with passion and devotion to truth is a primary responsibility. But doing so in the context of love is a greater responsibility.

Insanity or Compassion?

I want to illustrate this concept briefly with a situation we are seeing in California. At this moment, there is a group of political people who are trying to push a bill through our state legislature that basically says if a child feels as though his or her gender is different from the biological gender he or she was born with, the

---

*Charles Wesley, *Epistles to Moravians, Predestinarians and Methodists. By a Clergyman of the Church of England*, as found in "MS Epistles," Duke Divinity School, https://divinity.duke.edu/sites/divinity.duke.edu/files/documents/cswt/05_MS_Epistles.pdf, 49.

parents or caregiver will not be able to help that child by providing counseling. They are only allowed to affirm the child's new sexual orientation. The backers of this bill are so set on this that the bill will allow and empower the government to pay for the medical treatments necessary to change the child's gender, which, by the way, is irreversible.

This is insanity, disguised as compassion. It is the worst I have seen from any political group. This comes from the same people who think there are dozens of genders. "God created man in His own image, in the image of God He created him; *male and female He created them*" (Genesis 1:27, emphasis added). Ideas like this bill find approval through unsanctified mercy, disguised as compassion. Compassion is needed for all involved. Period. Let's be known for our love. But the moment believing a lie becomes a manifestation of approval, we are the most to be pitied.

These are not fringe lunatics on the edge of society. These are elected officials. Few things have angered me as much as this nonsense being pushed through ignorant political puppets. There is no excuse for this. When a culture removes the concept of a Designer, we lose all sense of design. When we no longer have a design, we lose accountability and purpose, and we are released to serve our own desires. Absolutes disappear, causing any remaining sanity to dissipate. This is when the perversion of the day is called normal, and those who oppose it are called "insensitive and uncaring." Yet one does not leave people in the second story of a burning building and say, "They are happy and sincere. We should leave them alone." Real love requires action.

This kind of insanity rules the day whenever a generation exalts human rights above human responsibilities. Responsibility automatically is accountability. And the bottom line is that people do not believe they will have to give an account of their lives to anyone. This is why *giving an account for our lives* is one of the foundational truths we must impart to our children. We will answer to God for what we have done with what we were given.

Use Your Brain

We must have parents who *think*, who are raising children who *think*, who are willing to get into the middle of the muck and bring change. It takes great discernment to wade through the deception offered by public opinion that was created by an agenda-driven media. And while the issue of discernment is critical, as is the mandate to find truth, an even greater challenge comes when we try to do this without making the people with the opposing view our enemy.

This is a scary endeavor if you have the need to please everyone all of the time, which of course is impossible. But many who stay out of controversy live in the illusion that they have favor. The absence of opposition is not favor. It is simply a form of peace that is not of the Kingdom, since it is based on something that is missing—conflict.

Those without an argument often demonize people with insight. People who oppose an issue because they hold a moral value are often called *extremists* by the Church, and are accused of *lacking compassion* by the unbeliever. Don't fall for unsanctified mercy. It is a counterfeit of the real thing, and it deadens us to love. It allows and applauds self-destructive behavior in the name of *not rocking the boat*. Real compassion shows great love and concern for the people who differ. There is also a willingness to work to understand the issue from their perspective. Such efforts bear great fruit in the long run.

If people refuse to see, their only recourse is to attack the credibility of their opponent. It is called a straw man argument, as it diverts attention away from the issue. My concern is for people who tend to be shaped by public opinion over biblical standards. The *thought police* of society use the lynch mob tactics of the Old West to condemn anyone who threatens their ideals.

Those who are bound by the fear of man have great difficulty taking a stand, as too much of their identity is wrapped up in the approval of others. Approval is important, as is the need to belong and to be loved and valued. Make sure to value the favor from people that is the result of favor from God.

This is of vital importance, but not just because of the issues involved. It is extremely important that we learn to think in a biblically sound way, without demonizing those who differ. By doing this well, we create a momentum for our children where they can learn to value truth, while at the same time loving those who think differently.

Raising Transformers

We are raising our children to change the world. Literally. To bring change well, they will need to understand culture, government, justice and education. It is vital for them to perceive the nature of biblical culture, which is the opposite of the politically correct mantra of the day. The politically correct approach is without Christ and sounds like wisdom, although it is the gibberish of fools. It is not that we need to become like another Israel. But it is vital for us to see how God says a society should function. Godly government is distinct in that by nature, it provides protection and empowerment. These things must become central to our children's ambition and strategy for how to bring change.

Chanting religious values, quoting Scriptures and the like do not bring change. I am not saying the Bible has no power. That certainly would be wrong. It is just that it is tough to inspire people for change when we quote a book they hold no value for. What these people do value is fruitfulness. It is possible, however, for us to proclaim the principles of God's Kingdom to them without ever quoting a Scripture.

Please understand, I am not trying to become popular. That has very little value to me. Nor am I interested in watering down truth by hiding the Word of God. But I am deeply committed to efficiency and wisdom. Efficiency is found in the fact that truth bears fruit, and it is hard to deny that Kingdom principles work wherever we have the authority to demonstrate them. Wisdom is found in that God alone understands the true building blocks of a society that will last. Study them. Proclaim them. Model them in whatever measure of rule you have in your life.

It is possible to live powerfully in a transformational way, bringing the wisdom of God's world into this one, serving with power for the miraculous, and still never really become religious. If we work entirely with churched people, or with those who have a cultural value for the Bible, quoting Scripture is powerful. It just does not work with those people who think it is archaic in nature.

What I like about the idea of living a fruitful life in front of people is that we get to introduce them to the ways of the Kingdom in such a way that they become hungry for the King. I remind you of the Scripture "O taste and see that the LORD is good" (Psalm 34:8). *Taste* is experience. *See* is perception. What you taste will influence what you see. It is the experience that often opens us up to a change in perception. Doing this for the unbeliever is a brilliant way to bring people to Jesus in a godless world. Let them taste of the reality of His love and His rule. It will change what they see and how they think.

One More Thing

It is essential that our children learn biblical government from us, since very few schools teach it anywhere. Understand it for yourself so you might at least plant seeds that can grow as your children enter adulthood and eventually come into position to spark change. The Kingdom of God, which is the way of life, is very attractive and *biblically* logical, if displayed correctly. And when displayed correctly, it brings forth fruit that is desirable to all.

I did not write this chapter so I could vent, or so I could highlight the ills of society. I find both of those approaches short-lived in effect and nauseating in experience. We are not to be ignorant of problems, of course, since we live in the middle of such decline. Yet I am looking for our children to become the voice of reason for their generation.

Neither do I write these things so we can argue about them and protest. That approach to life is very unfulfilling, falling short of our assignment. While drawing attention to what is wrong has merit, it is seldom a focus for what I am assigned to do.

I write these things with hope for the big picture. I write them so that our children and our children's children will be armed with insight, love, wisdom and power—so they will bring about lasting change to the cities and nations of the world. Our children will be given places of great influence because of how they were raised. I long to see them burn with conviction in response to their God-given place in life.

I write with hope for a better future.

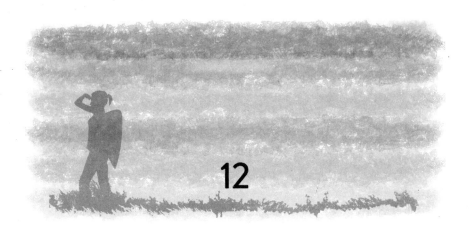

Revival unto Reformation

T HE ISSUES I ADDRESSED in the previous chapter about government and such are worthy of a book of their own, but
not one I want to write. I would, however, like to add a few
thoughts to identify the real hope for all our nations. The obvious
answer to our need is Jesus, an answer that has been applied in different ways throughout history. Sometimes the change that comes
is lasting. And sometimes it is a short-lived spiritual activity that has
very little lasting effect, except on those who were saved. Salvation
is the ultimate change. But tragically, the power of transformation
often stays confined to the four walls of the Church.

When the move of God fails to have an impact on culture itself,
we are left with dove's dung. Dove's dung represents what is left after
the dove has moved on: "There was a great famine in Samaria; and
behold, they besieged it, until a donkey's head was sold for eighty
shekels of silver, and a fourth of a kab of *dove's dung* for five shekels
of silver" (2 Kings 6:25, emphasis added). The dove in Scripture represents the Holy Spirit, who came upon Jesus in power at His water
baptism. It says that the dove remained on Him (see Luke 3:22). Jesus
modeled an ongoing move of God that changed everything because

of this abiding presence. The dung is what is left, however, when the dove is gone—that is, when the Holy Spirit is no longer involved in our lives, churches and ministries.

God's intention in every revival is far greater than to have us as believers experience a brief boost in our faith. I am Pentecostal through and through, and I am very thankful for my heritage. It is heartbreaking to see that some of the great Pentecostal moves of God lasted only a few months or years and had very little long-term influence. Certainly, the countless numbers of people who were born again during those revivals were forever changed. Yet very little transformation took place in the cities and nations those people were part of. This should never be okay with us. In my estimation, every revival has the seeds of reformation in it, if those who are affected by the outpouring of the Spirit would learn to translate the effects into practical daily living.

What are you raising your children for? What is their purpose for being? Of course, it is to love God and His people. And yes, it is to be faithful and be good witnesses. We want them to be successful in every part of their lives. That is a given. But what does God want from this generation? What is the target we are raising them to aim for that will have great impact on their world? I believe we should learn about and be exposed to great moves of God. In doing that, we will learn how to see change come to society itself through these outpourings of the Spirit.

Highs and Lows of Church Attendance

It has been proven that, at least in the United States, the cities with the largest churchgoing population have the worst social statistics. I would never assume that church attendance is the problem, nor would I ever believe that crime or divorce increases because people attend church. But it does present a challenge for people who attend a vibrant church and assume that because there is such life within the building and its programs, that in itself is affecting their city. That simply is not the case. I don't think the devil minds if we have good meetings, are excited about church and love being together. Just as long as we don't take those opinions and perspectives into the community, where they will have the greatest impact.

It is common for the church attenders to think that the answer to their city's ills is to get people into their buildings. I love the fact that people can attend our great churches and have their lives changed. The real problem, however, is that we want them to come in instead of our going out.

The answer is not even more powerful outreaches, as much as I love those activities. The answer is people who are passionately in love with Jesus, who believe God has answers for every issue in society. From that place of burning conviction, we go out to be the leaven in the lump of dough, where change is then inevitable.

Taking Responsibility

I think that perhaps the biggest challenge when we find a group of people who love their local church is to get them to adopt the issues that surround them in their cities. I know for us at Bethel, we love being together. As one of our staff members said, "I love us." Me, too. Our greatest strength is that we don't need anyone.

Yet that is also our greatest weakness. Redding has a great church-attending population. We also have bold ministers of the Gospel in the everyday saints who take the love of God to the streets of our cities. In some ways, we excel there. But we also have great homelessness and crime. There are reasons for this that I don't need to address here. What is important to speak of here and now, however, is that a genuine move of God has the elements for societal transformation embedded in its DNA.

To be contributors to the well-being of our cities, we must take on responsibility in prayer and action to bring betterment to our regions. One of the most practical ways we can do this in the long term is by being intentional about how we raise our children. We must raise them with divine purpose.

The Jesus People Movement

I remember so well the Jesus People movement of the seventies. It was a most remarkable thing to see thousands and thousands of young people turning to Jesus. Chuck Smith became one of the primary fathers of that movement. He had an unwavering love for hippies, regardless of their dress or smell. When many wanted dress codes posted at the door of the church, Pastor Chuck welcomed all who were willing to come. It really was a remarkable time. The anointing for evangelism was so strong that you could almost say anything and people wanted to give their lives to Jesus. We owe a great debt of gratitude to Chuck Smith and the others like him who lent their strength to that great move of God.

As remarkable as that season was, there was a fly in the ointment. Probably several, but the one I want to mention here is the fact that a large part of the Church was expecting Jesus to return at any moment. The signs of the times certainly pointed to the fact, since the days were dark, with increasing evil seemingly everywhere. I don't oppose the theology of the return of Christ. I firmly believe that He is coming back and that we don't know when. My problem is not with the idea of His return. It is with the Church's response to that promise, where believers think it removes them from the responsibility to bring transformation.

We had a generation of brilliant young leaders who converted during that movement. But they did not want to go to university, because Jesus would be coming at any time and they thought it would be better to evangelize instead. They thought that school would be a waste of time. It sounded so good—except it was not. It robbed society of seeing what could happen to a generation if sold-out lovers of Jesus would enter a variety of professions so they could represent Him well in bringing wholeness to our cities and nations.

Some of our best and brightest did not pursue excellence in training for this reason. If that were not tragic enough, those without

Christ did pursue their goals and ambitions, which positioned the ungodly to become today's professors in our colleges, judges in our judicial system and mayors of our cities. At a time when we most needed a generation of Jesus lovers to pursue their place of influence in life, they were elsewhere, waiting for Jesus to return. We have to find a way to lovingly anticipate the Lord's return without forfeiting our responsibility to "occupy until He comes" (see Luke 19:12–14).

I believe that this is one of the greatest tragedies in Church history. We really had a generation of zealous new believers positioned to grow in their calling and bring about societal change through becoming excellent in their professions. They would have been in place to pass laws that upheld righteousness. They could have taught a generation what moral values and responsibility look like from their honored positions in the university. They would have ruled with a servant's heart from their place of political influence. But it did not happen. In many of this world's systems today—educational, judicial, political, medical and more—the ungodly rule. The devil planned ahead. We did not. It is tragic.

Help, I'm a Parent!

I know that my appeal to you as a parent may be a bit overwhelming at times, but please follow this through. You have a gift that is to impact the nations of the world—your child. He or she has the potential and assignment to kill the giants of our day. It is not that every child can become president, or that all of them can become heart surgeons or star athletes or the next Billy Graham. But everyone has a role to play in bringing about the purposes of God in the earth—that all the kingdoms of this world would belong to Him. Completely.

The spiritual wake your children leave behind has little to do with their title in life and everything to do with the depth of their character and the nature of their *yes* to God. We are to help our children

151

answer the questions as to why we are here, what our assignment is and what His purpose is in the earth. Everyone can and must leave a mark in this regard.

While I want to see our children become the lawyers and judges of the next generation, I also want them to become the CEOs who know excellence, compassion and creativity as they influence the value system of the big business of our nation (or yours). I want to see them in the political offices of the nations. We need them to live in absolute surrender and undefiled in their approach to service, to become the leaven within those sometimes corrupt environments.

We need these things for our children and for ourselves. But if we only measure our children's success by their job title or the awards they receive in recognition of their gifts, we will have fallen short. Esther, Daniel and Joseph were all people of the Bible for whom we have great respect. But none of them were the president, prime minister, queen or king of their nations. Yet their *yes* to God spared several nations from certain doom, releasing them into their divine destinies. Each of these leaders was given the privilege to serve the person who was at the top of the political structure, instead of being number one himself or herself. From their hidden place of influence, nations were changed.

Parent or grandparent, you are the leader of God's most practical and powerful government on the planet. The family reigns supreme. And while there are many days when survival seems to be a good enough goal, please never lose sight of what is possible in your lifetime. It is possible to raise up a generation of children who know what the power of God looks like and how to operate in it, and yet have the wisdom to help shape the value system of their nation for decades to come. The revival, the wonderful outpouring of the Holy Spirit, must be translated into reformational impact. We owe the world a glimpse of what it looks like to have King Jesus rule with power and purpose. This is our privileged responsibility.

152

Calvin and the Guys

We recently celebrated the five-hundred-year anniversary of the Reformation. When the Lord first began to stir my heart for this subject, I was deeply impacted by this group of spiritual leaders who influenced the culture of a society when given the chance. I have not read of any power-filled meetings where the sick were healed and the dead were raised. It may have happened, but that was not what they were known for. What they experienced would not qualify for what many of us might consider a great move of God, compared to our own experience. And yet they influenced centuries of world history. This is extraordinary.

This provoked me so deeply that I arranged to spend a couple of days in Geneva, the city deeply associated with the Reformation, just to examine this phenomenon. What I came away with was quite convicting. These spiritual leaders brought about change because they believed that God has answers for every issue of life. They believed that He has a way to do banking, education, medicine and more. The point is, God is practical, and sometimes we are not. The spoil went to those who believed that God has answers. They taught these answers and applied them to their lives. Doing so shaped their world with His insights for life. This created a blessing over a region of the world that still has influence on the world around it. The United Nations, the World Bank, the YMCA, Rolex, Cartier and many other institutions of excellence and human service are either headquartered in Geneva or have main branches there. The seeds of significance were planted centuries ago.

We are raising children with purpose. One of the easiest things in the world is to lose sight of the big picture, because we get so overwhelmed by the season they are in—from their time in diapers, to their runny noses, to their challenging Little League schedules, to the temptations they face in high school. In those seasons, it is work as parents to keep mindful of why, how and what. The point is, there is a lot of stuff going on in all our families. But we owe it to our children and the world around us to remain conscious of the big picture. We are raising giant-killers who will have an effect on the course of world history. Pray it. Quote it. Sing it. Declare it. *We are raising giant-killers who will have an effect on the course of world history!*

Sexuality by Design

G OD IS THE FATHER of life. All life. He created this world for
His pleasure and for ours. He delights in all He has made,
giving us access to that same joy. We behold beauty, day after
day, all because God delights in our enjoyment of what He has made.
He did not create food just to give us energy and health. He designed
it to include bringing us pleasure. As I write, I am remembering
the peaches I get delivered to my house every week throughout the
summer months. Sweet organic peaches—pure pleasure! This is the
nature of our Father and the design He has for every part of our lives.
Trusting the Designer is the smartest move any of us could make.

God creates rules and behavioral boundaries to protect life. He
does not give them because He is against our joy or pleasure. Quite
the opposite. The boundaries that God has given us for life are there
to protect His goal for us—ultimate pleasure, both now and in eternity. Sin has pleasure, but only in the moment. Righteous living has
sustainable pleasure throughout a lifetime.

I love Proverbs 10:22, "It is the blessing of the LORD that makes
rich, and He adds no sorrow to it." When the breakthroughs of life
come from the hand of God, they don't come with sorrow attached.
There is no balloon payment at the end that makes us regret our

decision to obey God. The principle involved in this verse is important to understand. If my "richness" comes from my hand, whether it is through dishonest financial gain, sexual sin or self-promotion, it comes with a cost. Always. There is always sorrow attached to pleasure outside of God's design. It is not punishment. The pain is caused whenever we violate design. In this case, the pain and sorrow of sin are the reminders that we are not God, we cannot design our own way and we must adhere to His purpose to discover why we are alive. Once again, He created us with specific purpose, both for His pleasure and for ours.

The Joy of Sex

God created sex to be enjoyed. Sex is both for procreation and for pleasure. But God also created the setting or context for sex. It is to be enjoyed only in the covenantal relationship called marriage between a man and a woman. Anything that differs from this is sin. It may lead to immediate pleasure, but it will cost. Sin is very expensive.

Kris Vallotton, the founder of Moral Revolution, reminds us that the first one to teach on a subject creates the standard by which all new information is measured. This means that when parents build a healthy sexual environment, teaching their children the place and purpose for our sexuality, what the kids then hear from educators and friends will be held against the standard their parents have already set.

Unfortunately for many parents, they wait until their children have already been indoctrinated into the subject of sex by an ungodly system. Then their instruction and insights become measured against what the child has already been taught. It becomes an uphill battle from there.

Purity, with a Ring to It

As my boys grew in both maturity and development, I took them out individually for a special dinner. Beni did the same thing for Leah.

We drove from Weaverville to Redding for this special one-on-one meal. Once again, we discussed our sexuality with them and why God gave us a sex drive. Where there is shame over sexual desire and sexuality, that shame drives people into secret practices. You don't want that as a parent. You want a sense of openness and honesty, where you can talk about these things with your children. We were very intentional about setting that kind of atmosphere with our kids, and taking them out for this special meal and conversation was part of that.

It is a lie to think that a sex drive defines or controls us. We are not defined by our temptations. Resisting the things that are outside God's purpose and plan strengthens us. And that strength will show up in many unrelated areas of life as we learn what to say yes to. Self-control is not merely the ability to say no to something wrong. It is the total commitment to the right *yes* that leaves little strength for anything contrary.

Living with self-control in our sexual appetite is a beautiful thing. When we get married, we are then able to give ourselves to our spouse completely in a way that no other person has enjoyed with us. On that special night, we give our spouse something that we have fought to protect—our sexual purity. The wedding night gift of purity is beautiful. It is both priceless and worth protecting.

After our talk, I gave each of my boys a very special ring to signify their covenant before God and before me. This purity ring was a physical reminder of an agreed-upon value for their lives.

As parents, we are not there to kill the joy of maturing or dating for our children. We are there basically to say, "What you want in life is a joyful marriage. And this is what it takes to have one."

The Purpose and Standards for Dating

There is so much built into our present-day culture that leads people toward a sexual experience. Dating should not mirror this false standard set by an ungodly society. Sex is for marriage. Period.

Because we care for our children, Beni and I set standards for their dating. Interestingly, many people have come to Beni through the years to ask her for those standards. As I mentioned earlier, Brian's friends would come home with him to discuss these issues with his mom. She became a champion of all things right and pure. She was so good at this topic that to this day, people still ask her about setting up biblical standards for dating. Someone will tell a friend, "You need to talk to Beni. She'll help you know what to do."

Here are the standards Beni and I set with our children for dating:

1. Never be alone in the house with a person of the opposite sex.

2. Do nothing that will create an expectation or appetite for a sexual encounter or experience. Whether it is a movie you are watching, or a physical touch, stay away from creating an expectation for something that is wrong.

3. Be involved in healthy activities with other like-minded people. Tragically, many who confess Christ live with a very low moral compass. As much as possible, stay away from people who don't affirm your values, especially in dating.

4. No French kissing. It is a wonderful way to kiss, but it causes sexual arousal. Beni and I determined early in our premarital relationship to stay away from that. Sexual arousal before marriage creates a false standard for a healthy relationship. Sex is extremely important in marriage, but as important as it is, it is a very small part of the relationship. Work to build communication skills.

5. Be wise. Be involved in activities that reinforce the goals of healthy dating, while at the same time avoiding sexual temptation. Being together in public places is good, especially at church activities and the like. Beni and I probably had only two actual dates in our two years before marriage. We spent time at her home with her family present, or we were involved in activities with other believers. Church and family environments are good.

The purpose of dating is to explore the personality, values, heritage and ways of thinking of the person you are interested in. You do not have to have the same backgrounds or personalities. It is more fun if there is diversity. But that diversity had better be with understanding, or there will be problems. Understanding and valuing differences goes a long way in building a relationship of trust where good communication is the norm.

Once a couple is headed for the altar, one or both may say, "We're getting married anyway, so let's have sex now." Listen, it is still wrong. And if someone will violate the law of God before marriage, likely he or she will do so after marriage, through adultery. In the cases where those standards have been broken, there is forgiveness. But there also must be healing of the issue that caused the failure in the first place. Deep sins need deep repentance.

The Act of Marriage

When two people engage in sexual intercourse, they become one. This beautiful mystery was created for marriage. Unity and oneness is God's desire for every couple that stands at the altar. It is the nature of God Himself—Father, Son and Holy Spirit. As such, it is His design for those of us who are married.

This wonderful mystery of life is to be treasured for what it is— God's design. It is in this context that we discover how marriage is meant to illustrate Jesus and His love for His Bride, the Church (people). Marriage in the natural is meant to be the shadow of this greater reality. Jesus loves the Church and gave Himself for her.

Upon our conversion, we were made one with God. That reality illustrates the beauty of marriage. The desire of the Lord is for the home to be the healthy environment known in heaven. This is where the husband and wife live in unity, and their children are raised in that atmosphere. As I said earlier, godly offspring are the result and were God's goal from the beginning (see Malachi 2:15).

The frightening part of this equation comes up when we look at those who commit adultery. In an immoral lifestyle, people give away a part of themselves, over and over again. When a man joins himself to a harlot, he is joining the Christ in him to that harlot. The thought of this should terrify every real believer, since it brings defilement to the undefiled—the name of Jesus. Is this not the warning 1 Corinthians 6:12–20 gives? I believe it is. While it is impossible to make the name of Jesus unholy through our actions, the mere thought of violating the privilege of being one with Christ should have a sobering effect on any believer who is considering such an immoral option. The same warning against such a mixture is taught in 1 Corinthians 10:21–22: "You cannot drink the cup of the Lord and the cup of demons; you cannot partake of the table of the Lord and the table of demons. Or do we provoke the Lord to jealousy? We are not stronger than He, are we?"

Rules from Love

When my children were small, we lived on Highway 299, which went from Eureka on the coast of California through Weaverville, to Redding and beyond. It was only a two-lane highway, but it was busy with potentially dangerous traffic. Logging was a big industry in that area since forests surrounded us. As a result, I created rules for my children's safety.

It was always my desire for my children to obey me because they knew I was wise and was always looking out for their best interests. It was pure logic to tell them they were not allowed to cross that highway. I could only imagine my five- to ten-year-old kids trying to navigate the dangers on that road. It was a formula for disaster. So my instruction to them went something like this: "Do not cross that highway. If you try to, and you actually live through the experience, you will have to answer to me when you return."

One day a friend of mine stopped by the house to talk. He was the undersheriff for our county. He told me that he had just had to swerve on that highway to miss hitting a child—mine. One of my boys had violated my rule. I sincerely thanked my friend for letting me know, and then I had a "meeting" with my son. It never happened again.

It really did not matter to me if, as a result of my standards, my children thought I was unkind or unfair, or did not understand them. I wanted them to live. To help with that, I established in their minds an awareness of the consequences for disobedience. And if they disobeyed and lived, and if there were no consequences, then there was a chance that they would continue to disobey until they died.

God's laws and rules are to protect life. They are to protect love. He is a much better Father in every possible way. He builds in us an awareness of consequences and rewards. Staying aware of those things and helping our children stay aware of those things give us all a wonderful advantage in life.

Our Standards

We had strict standards over how we did life in our home. And while this next standard may not be important to you, it was to us. We did not allow any secular music in our home. I don't apologize for that at all. I know how music affected me in my early years, and I decided against having my family influenced by secular lyrics. That was a decision I made. In fairness, I have a lot of family and friends who think completely differently, and I have complete respect for them since they are able to monitor that issue quite well in their households.

The thing I am concerned about is that when we listen to music or watch a movie, we sometimes unconsciously receive from someone else's imagination. The imagination is wonderful—when influenced by Kingdom values. In fact, the imagination yielded to God becomes the sanctified imagination. It is the yielded imagination that is positioned for visions and dreams. But sometimes we are exposed to a very ungodly imagination on the screen or in a song. I do not throw my standard out as a law, whatsoever. Just live aware.

We chose to live with strict standards in our household from the early days. Rather than allowing a lot of secular influence, we focused our hearts on what the Lord was blessing. We were being intentional. Whatever standards you set, make sure you protect your family from unnecessary ungodly influence. That is the point. You may allow all kinds of things, but just make sure you monitor the attitudes and values your family members might adopt because of the impact of what you have allowed into your home.

Shame and Design

There is no shame in godly sex. Shame is unavoidable outside of God's design. Much of the fight and animosity in this area come from people trying to blame the Church and/or society for creating moral standards with which they disagree. Yet day by day, these people violate their design. Shame is unavoidable in that case, because the law of God is written in their hearts. Moral values are not externally imposed standards; they are an expression of conscience.

The only way to become shame-free is to live with purity. The only other way is to continue in sin until your conscience is seared. Little by little, the persistent violator's heart dies as a result.

A prevailing thought throughout all of life must be that we will give an account for our lives (see 2 Corinthians 5:9–11). It may seem as though I am beating that drum too much. But there is a day coming when people will wish they had heard of this day of accounting more often. Being reminded of it is not meant for the purpose of manipulating the hearts of our children or others through fear. It is a gift from God that enables us to live with wisdom. It is to help us create responsible lifestyles.

The way we live in our homes, holding each other accountable with mercy and grace, gives a context in which our children will learn what God values in a healthy environment. Sexuality is a wonderful subject, if kept in divine perspective. It is divisive and perverse outside that context.

Homosexuality

Homosexuality is becoming a major issue throughout the Church. Those in this movement—and it is political in nature—have successfully turned public opinion in their favor through a decades-long strategy. They were happy with small victories, but always had their sights on being in charge. But their newfound popularity does not make it right.

Loving people, regardless of their issues, is our number one assignment. Agreeing with their opinions or lifestyles is not necessary in order for us to show them real love. We must know how to love without rejecting the people with whom we disagree. But it is equally important not to succumb to the pressure of agreeing with what is wrong, that we might show compassion. So much of what God is doing in the earth will be destroyed if we give up on this homosexuality issue. It is the fly in the ointment. Some of the finest material I know of on this subject is found in Kris Vallotton's Moral Revolution books and online teachings.*

Jesus is returning for a Bride, not a boyfriend. Once we remove the Creator from the consciousness of society, we become lawless, since our purpose and design no longer have any merit. Our physical design testifies to God's intent. He created us male and female. There are two genders. And those who think otherwise need compassion and help. But for us to agree with them is to violate God—His nature, His Word and His creation.

In today's school systems, our children likely will be exposed to other kids who are struggling with gender identity issues. Oftentimes, the gender issue is demonically inspired and the enemy comes into weak places. Sometimes child sexual abuse, fatherlessness, porn or other issues are involved. If your kids have friends who are struggling, they can offer compassion and prayer, without agreeing with those friends about the underlying issues. Help your kids understand what is at work behind the scenes, so they can be a redemptive

*For more information, visit https://moralrevolution.com.

solution to their friends. But they need to understand that there are male and female—there is not any other option. Your children can speak to the good they see in a struggling friend. Finding the gold in people and speaking to that works in these kinds of contexts.

Experts in sin will always make their point of view look appealing. Appealing to our conscience to get us to show compassion does this. So many believers don't know how to love with compassion without agreeing with the point of view of the person being loved. And the present political climate has not helped this challenge at all. Disagreeing with a position invites all kinds of attacks and slanderous comments. Many people cannot withstand such pressure, so they yield to the lies.

Loving without Offense

One of the greatest challenges in our lives is to love people well, without picking up their offenses. Can you serve college students without being offended at a political party? Can you serve the poor without becoming offended at big business? Can you serve the rich without becoming offended at people who will not work? Can you serve children without becoming offended at adults who do not make them a priority? Can you serve adults without becoming offended at the teenager who shows them no respect? Can you serve in foreign missions without being offended at the rich in the Church who have little vision for taking the Gospel worldwide? Can you serve one race without being offended at another, and vice versa?

This list of questions is almost without end. The challenge before us is big. Having compassion for people in their pain is one of our most treasured assignments. Love them without judgment. And be immovable in biblical truth. Your agreement with people is not a necessary requirement in order to show them love.

As sexuality becomes redefined by the latest perversion of the day, we have to be more resolved in protecting what is right, without partnering with the political spirit to obtain a moral victory.

Those with the political spirit use manipulation tactics to threaten and persuade people to their way of thinking. Truth is appealing to those who love truth. Do not use Scripture to beat up the offender. There is no reward for being right. But there is a reward for loving those who do not love you in return.

Sex was intended for pleasure, according to God's design and within the context He designed it for. Raising children to embrace God's design for our sexuality positions them for living the ultimate lifestyle of joy, pleasure and fulfillment in this area. The purpose behind biblical training is not only to keep our children away from the things that destroy, but also to enable them to enter fully into the life of pleasure that God has willed for each married person. This is sexuality done well, and it must be the goal of every parent to protect and empower his or her children in this area.

14

Exposure to World Need

Exposure to radiation is extremely dangerous and life threatening. For example, long-term exposure to even small amounts of radiation dramatically increases the risk of cancer. Exposure to large amounts, even for a brief period of time, can lead to radiation sickness, with symptoms like nausea, skin burns, hair loss and even reduced organ function. Radiation is deadly.

I realize that this is a strange way to open a chapter in a book about raising children to change the world. But I cannot find a better example of the concept of exposure. What if I told you there were things more powerful than radiation, but that they had positive effects on a child instead of negative ones? Understanding this enables us to be more intentional in our parenting, knowing that selectively exposing our children to the right things has tremendous effect on their lives.

To make this illustration work, you will have to shift from thinking of the negative effects of exposure to what it would be like if there was an equally effective element that brought about a positive effect on people simply through the right exposure. In other words, the kind of exposure I am talking about is even more powerful than radiation, but it changes people for the better.

Exposure to the Kingdom of God is the element that is far greater in impact. It is leaven that causes all it comes into contact with to rise under its influence. It will have eternal impact on those who are exposed to the real deal. We must learn to teach and train our children through the right kinds of exposure.

Compassion Is the Norm

We Americans live in a nation that is very privileged. It does not mean everybody is rich and famous here. But it does mean we have access to things that, as you travel around the world, you realize quite quickly that not everybody has access to. Beni and I did not want to raise children who had entitlement issues, where they felt that the world owed them, so we determined early on that we wanted to expose them to world need.

When you see somebody in pain, it is normal to hurt. It is normal for us to weep with those who weep. It is normal for a child to want to give all his toys away when he sees a kid who lives in poverty. That is normal. It proves our kids are alive. They don't have to be taught that.

It is important for us to model compassion in our households, but it is already in our children's hearts. It is important to recognize what God has already put in your children, and then to expose them to the environments that will cause it to come to the surface and eventually mature.

You always want to keep things in front of your children so that their heart of compassion is never dead or callous.

Poverty and Pain

As I already mentioned, for many years we lived on the main highway that went through Weaverville, California. Because of our location, people passing through town would often stop by to ask for help with food, gas money or sometimes a place to stay. We would always try to do our best to help in any situation that would arise.

It was somewhat common for my children to wake up in the morning and see a stranger sleeping on our living room floor. That stranger would then join us for breakfast before heading on his or her way. My children never felt fear about this, because I was always there to protect them should the need arise.

The safety of my family is my primary concern and responsibility, so praying for discernment in these moments is critical. There are some people you should never invite into your home when children are present. That being said, we chose to serve broken people and expose our children to their immediate needs of food and shelter. While our reason for serving these people was to love them as God did, it also had a great effect on our children. I owed them exposure to the needs of people who would never be able to pay us back. It was important to put the kids in a position where their hearts would be stirred with compassion. This is my obligation to them. Isolating our children from the pain of other people is an unacceptable way to live.

One unmarried couple received Christ while passing through town. Beni and I performed their wedding in our living room. Kris and Kathy Vallotton were there as witnesses. I have done many weddings in my forty-plus years of pastoring, and I don't remember any wedding as powerful as that one. God's presence filled our home in such a beautiful and powerful way that it marked me forever.

This couple ended up moving into our home for a season in their newly married life. We did not bring them in to live with us so that our children could learn a lesson on kindness or hospitality. It was for the couple, entirely. But our children always benefit when we live life in the open, as unto the Lord. Life itself becomes the lesson.

Missions

Almost every summer for many years, we took our children to work in an orphanage called Rancho de Sus Niños, in Tecate, Mexico. In fact, our oldest son, Eric, lived and volunteered there for a season after high school. This ministry not only has an orphanage; they also have a school for children, and they plant churches and train people for ministry in their Bible school. It is a most unusual ministry because of its wide variety of ministries, along with its breadth of influence. It also recently expanded its ministry into Romania.

Our children worked on the always-expanding facilities of this ministry with manual labor. They also took great joy in playing with the children in the orphanage. A notable highlight for all of us was taking food and clothing to the people who lived in the nearby dump. Absolute poverty reigned over these dear people. They would try to make a living by going through the garbage to find things they might be able to use or sell. It was heartwrenching to see. They were so receptive of our efforts to help them, and so thankful.

It is painful to see people in this kind of need. We cannot afford to be ignorant of such need, nor can we become callous to these people's pain. Having your heart hurt in this way shows you are still alive. Most people insulate themselves from such uncomfortable feelings, but that is a luxury I cannot afford. Beni and I were deliberate in exposing ourselves and our children to the needs of others. As a family, we needed to remain conscious of and exposed to human need. This was an important part of our strategy in raising our children. The compassion muscle needs to be exercised, not protected from use. Intentional exposure is essential.

This was only one small part of our commitment to worldwide missions. I was raised to greatly value the spreading of the Gospel to the nations of the world. It is so important to give financial and prayer support to the parts of the world where we can receive no direct benefit for our gift. As the great missionary statesmen C. T. Studd, Jim Elliot and others have said, "The light that shines the farthest shines the brightest at home." Giving attention to the international cry for help does not weaken the brilliance of the light of the Gospel in our own city. It magnifies it, as God shouts "Yes!" to us embracing our assignment in life.

Eric was also part of a group of young people who smuggled Bibles into China. He had just turned fifteen at the time. At the age of fourteen, Brian went with me on a mission trip to India. While in her early teens, Leah was part of a team that brought the Gospel to the streets of Spain. It took incredibly hard work and courage on Leah's part to minister on the streets in song in a language she did not know. Her heart for the nations gave her the courage to do so with great skill. She did it so well that people thought she spoke Spanish.

The point is, the need of hearing the Gospel message, and the pain of poverty and disease, give us opportunities to serve people who will never be able to pay us back. The common idea is that the need is so big that we will never be able to fix the problem. And that is so true. But we can touch someone. And we must. It may be that the absence of finances or good opportunities makes international trips impossible at this time for your household. Then serve at the local rescue mission, or serve meals to the homeless. Do something.

Building an awareness in our children of the world's need to hear the Gospel is a huge part of our responsibility as parents. Giving them firsthand experience helps multiply the effect of our words regarding missions by about a thousand times. This is my debt to my children. As I write this, I am sending one of my oldest granddaughters on a mission trip to Brazil with my dearest of friends, Randy Clark, of Global Awakening Ministries. She will join a team of youth who have given themselves to serve, preach and pray for the sick.

Foster Children

Another part of our attempt to expose our children to world need was to invite foster children to live with our family. The generosity and compassion of my daughter, Leah, made this possible, since she would give up her bedroom for a season so that the foster children would have a room of their own.

The most tragic case we fostered involved two little boys whose mother had killed herself because of the abuses she had suffered.

Within a year or so, the father did the same. There were actually five boys in all, of which we cared for two. To say they were traumatized is an understatement, as you can imagine. They received weekly counseling provided by the childcare service in our county. I am thankful that such services are available for children in need.

It was interesting to see how these two boys, around four and six years of age, sat with us at the dinner table for the first time. They grabbed all the food they could reach and wrapped their arms around it so no one else could have any. It became obvious that they had not always had food, and that they had survived by looking out for themselves. We assured the boys that they could have all the food they wanted and that there would be more tomorrow.

These boys' lives began to change immediately, and they were released from the need for counseling only a few weeks after entering our home. This was an extraordinary miracle in our thinking, because the kinds of issues they had are so deeply rooted. It is also a testimony to the impact of God's love on the heart of a child as he or she enters a safe home. The child heals completely.

Our homes are supposed to be places of safety and refuge. Life is not fair, and not everyone is kind, considerate or respectful. But home is the place where every family member returns to be strengthened and empowered for the next day. That is the beauty of family. It is the one place where everybody belongs.

Avoiding Pain

If there ever was a culture that avoided pain, it would be the culture of this present day. I heard a talk show on the radio years ago in which a psychologist was being interviewed. He mentioned to the host that in his opinion, a very large percentage of mental illness is caused by the attempt to avoid pain. That is an extremely significant statement. No one likes pain, nor should we. But avoiding what is normal in life can take you into places of great irresponsibility and denial.

Let me make something clear: I hate pain. Every kind there is. But without pain, a child would leave his or her hand on the hot stove, destroying a body part. Without pain, an athlete would keep running, possibly bringing about permanent damage to an injured body part. Without running the risk of emotional pain in a relationship, there is no chance to receive love. In the measure that I can experience pain, I can be loved.

It is wisest to use pain to our advantage. This starts with giving thanks in the middle of it, finding a biblical promise and solution. Confess and proclaim the promise of God, while making sure you are committed to doing whatever God said to do. We have confidence in God's desire and ability to bring justice into our lives, and that He will more than make up for it if anyone has treated us unjustly. And if our pain was caused by our own misdeed, God forgives and restores.

Raising our children to live like this will give them decades of advantage over just about anyone else their age. Most people live their entire lives without ever learning to monitor their hearts in this fashion. And yet it is the heart of a person that helps bring about the promotion only God can give.

Inconvenience Speaks

We have a Good Friday Easter Service in our city. Somewhere around one hundred churches are involved in this wonderful event every year. We have to hold multiple services to accommodate all those interested in attending. I plan my calendar around this day, since it is that significant for me.

Our Bethel folks are so extremely supportive of these kinds of events, and they testify of the great work God is doing in our city. There are so many great churches in Redding. We are so thankful for the privilege of serving our city by participating in this unifying event with so many wonderful leaders and their flocks. It is a beautiful honor for us.

I remember a couple of years ago, when I felt that because there is no childcare available at these special services, I needed to make a point to our church families about their attendance. The problem is that if you have children, attending such a large gathering can be challenging because your children may cry or get restless. I challenged our parents to train their children intentionally by choosing to take part in Kingdom-oriented activities like this that can be extremely inconvenient. That way, our children can watch and discover what we are willing to pay a price for.

Never underestimate your children's ability to recognize what you really value. Communicate the purpose of a meeting or other activities as they grow older. They will learn the importance of sacrifice and purpose through your example. If I value convenience, comfort and a life that never has pain, I have trained my child to take the easy road in life. Sometimes the simple act of inconvenience speaks more to a child, over time, than a hundred sermons on the importance of sacrifice.

Beni and I lived this way throughout our children's growing-up years. We still do. As David said, I will not offer God something that did not cost me (see 2 Samuel 24:24). Israel had this built into their culture. In Nehemiah 8 the whole family stood for hours, listening to the Word of God being read. In 2 Chronicles 20:13, the whole family was present to hear a prophetic word given to the nation during a time of great crisis: "All Judah was standing before the LORD, with their infants, their wives and their children." Even the babies were present, though they could not possibly have understood what was spoken. It is vital to illustrate to our children what is important to us, not because it is easy, but because it is right.

More Than a Skill Set

I love efficiency, and I love seeing things work smoothly in life. I also avoid all unnecessary pain and consider that normal and good. But pain does not scare me anymore—not if I know doing God's will causes it.

In the same way that children need seven positive comments to offset every one negative comment, so our children must be exposed to things that are right in contrast to the pain and needs of this world. If they are exposed only to need and tragedy, they will have little hope of changing it. But should they become anchored in their souls to the way of life that God intended, they will be less likely to cower in the face of insurmountable challenges. Promise, purpose and reward help bolster the hearts of those inclined to avoid such opportunities.

We are raising children not only to bring life and fix problems; we are raising a generation to be the solution to problems. We are instilling in them more than a skill set. The value system of God, established deep in our hearts, includes our access to His unlimited resources. Those resources enable us to be what is needed. As someone once said, "Don't try to be the best in the world. Try to be the best *for* the world."

There is a promise that rules over every part of our lives: "And we know that God causes all things to work together for good to those who love God, to those who are called according to His purpose" (Romans 8:28). That wonderful promise would not be necessary if everything worked the way we think it should. It is there because we face mystery, challenges, pain and need. Because of those things, God gave us a promise that must become our refuge. Kris Vallotton puts it this way: "All things work for good in the end. If it's not good, it's not the end."

God has the final say. Be quiet long enough to hear Him speak.

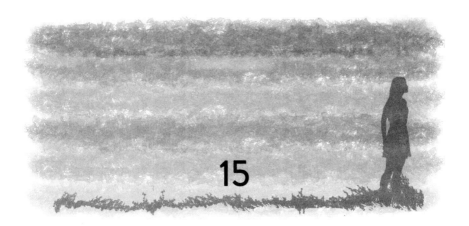

15

Exposure to Community

KEEP IN MIND the concept I shared at the start of chapter 14 about exposure to radiation, with all its negative effects. But then imagine once more a similar kind of exposure for our children to something very positive, with positive effect. That concept will once again be our model. It is our responsibility as parents to choose what to expose our children to for positive effect.

We cannot always protect our children from some of the ideas and practices of the world system apart from Christ. But we can be deliberate in bringing about their exposure to the realities of God's world that will leave an eternal imprint on their hearts. It is wisdom for us to recognize the kinds of things to expose our kids to that will bring lasting influence. As we saw in the previous chapter, exposing them to world need is one of those things. Another thing that I want to talk about here is exposing them to community.

The Culture of God

We in the Western Church tend to emphasize our individual relationship with God over the corporate. I do believe there is wisdom in this, as God has no grandchildren. We must be born again. And that does not happen to groups of people. It requires personal surrender.

On the other hand, much of what we need to learn is connected to our understanding of and practice at being "members of one another" (Romans 12:5). It is not either/or. It is both/and. This concept is vital for us to learn as adults, and then to pass on to our children. This is especially needed at this time, when computer games and social media are stealing the emotional energies necessary for us to experience the wealth involved in biblical community. Practically put, we need people. And our ability to do community can never go beyond the community we have in our household. Success at home gives us the authority base to go anywhere else. If I fail at home and succeed in touching the nations, I have failed. We do need each other, and it starts at home.

In the prayer Jesus taught His disciples, He started with "Our Father." If anyone could have said "My Father," it would have been Jesus. Yet His purpose was to emphasize something extremely significant—our inclusion in the family of God. This fits well into His lesson on loving God and people. We must love our neighbors as we love ourselves. Biblical *self-love* enables us to love others well.

Small Groups

We had home groups during all of our children's growing-up years, where believers gathered every week to pray, study and be together. Being in a home group was such a wonderful part of our growth as a family. It was a tool God used powerfully to shape my children's development as healthy contributors to society.

In these gatherings, we almost always shared a meal together with our friends, who varied in age from young married couples with small children to single adults to grandmas and grandpas. The point is, we intentionally gathered people of different age groups and backgrounds who would expand our ability to value and celebrate people different from ourselves. This really was a beautiful time of our week.

One of the things I loved to do in our small group was to pick a person for everyone to encourage. I would ask the rest of the group what they thought God was saying to this individual, and what marks of God's influence they saw on the person's life. Sometimes I would ask the group what they loved about that person. It was such a rewarding part of our time together, as we learned early on not to pick out any of the person's faults or shortcomings. A culture of honor celebrates who a person is, without stumbling over who he or she is not. During such times, people were so encouraged to find out the impact of their lives on those around them.

Much of what we did in these moments was based on a concept Ephesians 2:10 contains: "For we are His workmanship, created in Christ Jesus for good works, which God prepared beforehand so that we would walk in them." The word *workmanship* comes from another word from which we get our word *poem*. Whenever we bring encouragement to people, we are simply reading the poetry of God that He is writing on the pages of their lives. It is an ongoing masterpiece, and we have the privilege of reading it while it is being written. Teaching children this value is vital. It does not take long for them to learn the importance of this way of life, since they become exposed to the brightened countenance of the person who is being encouraged. It really is a beautiful thing.

Most people live aware of the things they wish were different in their lives, with a heightened awareness of their own weaknesses and idiosyncrasies. What many usually don't know is their significance, gifting or value to others. I often included our children in this group activity as we "called out the gold in people." People are like gold mines, where there is always more dirt and debris than there is gold. But there is a rich vein of gold in every life. The beauty is that we have the privilege of pointing to the gold. The children always functioned with brilliant accuracy and insight as they called out the gold in adults, as well as in others of their age group. I think this was one of the exercises we used in both our home and our relationships with others that helped our children learn to brag on each other instead of competing. Children who are secure in their identity are more likely to compliment another person.

Community Starts at Home

The way we value our friends helps our children understand the value of community. They must be exposed to the strength and beauty of meaningful relationships, or they will settle for online friends and computer games as real life. This is a critical issue to address in the day-to-day routine of life. Real friends make us better.

There is a wonderful African proverb that says, *If you want to go fast, go alone. But if you want to go far, go together.*

There is a time for solitude, and protecting that need will help a child know life is not a choice between one or the other—solitude or community. But much more can be accomplished when we learn to develop meaningful relationships with people who make us stronger and bring out the best in our lives. We can go much further in our impact on this world as we learn to do life together rather than trying to do everything by ourselves.

Likewise, when our children know what it is like to live in healthy relationships, they can then spot when relationships are demeaning or draining—one of the ways that our intentional parenting provides protection for them. We all need to be with people who celebrate us, not just tolerate us. Some of what we need to see about God and ourselves can only be discovered in a community.

The Honor of Community

My uncle, Ed Gunderson, died unexpectedly when I was around ten years old. He was married to my mother's sister and was a prince of a man. They were pastors in Minnesota. We drove there from our home in California to attend the funeral and serve his family. He and Aunt Gladys had three daughters, plus they had just adopted a little boy. They also had a niece living with them.

I had never seen people experience pain on that level before. As we drove up to the house, we could hear the loud weeping inside. It was rough. We often protect our children from discomfort or pain. Part of that is wisdom, as there is a limit to what we expose children to, especially when they are small. But it is also important for them to see life and see how to navigate the hard things. This is where families must talk through pain and pray together. We must allow questions, without the need for having a ready answer. As parents, sometimes we have answers. Oftentimes, we don't. Let the unanswered question take you as a family to God. Search the Scriptures and pray. What is gained through those kinds of problems is unforgettable. Navigate them well, always taking children to Jesus so they can hear from Him for themselves.

After the funeral, my mom and dad invited my uncle's remaining family members to move to California and live with us. They did. My grandparents were already part of our household, which made for quite a community, with eleven people living in a home of eleven hundred square feet.

Children adapt quite easily to building community. If you put children in a playground together with other children, they usually will build friendships quickly and easily. In our little home, all of us children thought it was fun to sleep on the floor or move into the garage during the summer months. Eleven people made it an adventure. I am sure my parents felt a bit more of the stress of that situation, but I never heard the slightest complaint from them, to this day. Community is an honor. We were blessed to have our family join us for that season, and we were honored to be able to help them.

Life Together

Community is not necessarily living together in a communal setting, although we have had many of those seasons through the years. Real community happens through communion. It is an issue of the heart. In this case, I am not referring to the Eucharist, where we partake of the body and blood of Jesus. Communion in this context is fellowship between members.

I like to define fellowship as *the exchange of life, from one member to another.* This is the process of true biblical growth and maturity. If I don't have deep, personal relationships with people, I can live with the illusion that I have all the fruit of the Spirit in my life (love, joy, peace, patience, kindness, goodness, faithfulness, gentleness and self-control). But when I make a meaningful connection with people, I come face-to-face with my need for growth. And it is not just that my need for maturity becomes apparent in relationships. Relationships are also the process God uses to sharpen me. "Iron sharpens iron" comes to mind for this concept (Proverbs 27:17). The very thing that exposes my need for maturity is what God uses to fulfill my need for maturity. It is found in the friendship where we learn to do life together.

Children who learn the secret of relationships and community will be miles ahead of their counterparts in all aspects of life, because our emotional intelligence (EI) is developed in a profound way through community. *Emotional intelligence* is considered the key to both personal and professional success in life. Psychologists have attributed EI to having healthy families, success in academics, a healthy self-esteem and thought life, and leadership skills. I never fault people for the size of their brain. But the size of someone's heart is entirely his or her responsibility. This is formed the best in community. And we owe exposure to this ongoing experience of community to our children. It is for their own development. The wonderful side benefit to having experienced community is the impact that people with the resulting EI from it have on the world around them.

There are parts of life that are best enjoyed in community. And sometimes that community is families living together. Kris and Kathy Vallotton have been part of our lives as the closest of friends for about forty years. At one time, they were building a home that was not ready when they needed it to be, so we invited them to move in with us. It was such an honor for us to have these friends live with us for a season. I am sure there must have been challenges with two families living together for an extended period of time, but I honestly don't remember any. I do remember when Kris and I were trying to find enough spare change to buy a gallon of ice cream for our two families to enjoy. Doing life together is an amazing honor.

The Sacrifice

We cannot understand the importance of this part of life until it costs us something. Its richness is found in sacrifice. That is in part what the writer of Hebrews was addressing in chapter 13, verses 15–16 (emphasis added):

> Through Him then, let us continually offer up a *sacrifice of praise* to God, that is, the fruit of lips that give thanks to His name. And do not neglect *doing good* and *sharing*, for with such *sacrifices* God is pleased.

Please notice the three New Testament sacrifices we are to make:

Praise—the fruit of the lips giving thanks for what God has done and honoring Him for who He is

Doing good—the good works we are to perform to benefit and serve others

Sharing—in the original language of Scripture, this is the word for "fellowship," the exchange of life one to another

Fellowship is one of the three sacrifices mentioned—the implication being that this part of life is to be sacrificial. In other words, meaningful relationships must cost us. If they remain only a convenient part of our life, we will never tap the riches of Christ that are hidden in the privilege of close relationships. Jesus can and must be discovered in the realm of community.

183

Community Provides

There is practical care in the context of community. I remember so many times that we were out of food and somehow my secretary, Barbara Calhoun, would know, although I never said a word. We would hear a knock at the door, and she would have bags and bags of wonderful groceries for us. She did not make much money as the church secretary in those days. I think she spent most of it on us. Thankfully, we are now the ones who are able to provide for those in need. This is what family does. Fellowship makes family practical. This is where we stand *with* and *for* one another. Our children benefit from this life lesson, probably more than any of us could possibly imagine.

I remember my boys would go to Barbara's office and ask for candy. She always seemed to have a private stash just for them. When Beni and I found out what they were doing, we put a stop to that. We told them it was not polite to ask for candy, so they stopped. We found out later that they changed their tactic and would go to her office and stand in front of her desk, completely silent. They did not say anything or ask for anything. They just looked at her, smiling.

Barbara looked at them one day, waiting for their request, but it never came. Being a rather perceptive one, she said, "Oh, were you told not to ask for candy?"

The boys nodded yes.

She then asked, "Would you like some?"

Of course, they said yes. They obeyed us perfectly and also got their candy. Ha! I have smart children.

Family gives. Family shares. Family learns together.

Accountability

Another of the rich tools God gives us in the context of community is accountability. This has been promoted much in recent days as a primary way for us to keep one another from sin. I am thankful for the emphasis on that, as it has inspired many to be willing to give an account of their private and personal lives. For example, if pornography is an issue for a man, being accountable helps. It has helped many leave that sinful habit. Knowing we have to give an account for our choices helps us live better. Plus, I believe it prepares us for one of life's greatest realities—that we will give an account of our lives to God.

While I love the idea of accountability to keep us from sin, I do believe its purpose is much higher. Accountability is giving an *account* for our *ability*. In other words, life together is not just about keeping one another out of problems. Community is to hold us to account for using our God-given abilities and gifts. Are we functioning according to our design?

Do you dream of writing? Is anyone holding you accountable for that dream? Are you taking classes on writing, attending seminars and reading the works of other great writers?

Do you want to start your own business? Is anyone holding you accountable for taking steps in that direction? Do you talk with business owners for advice, read books on the subject or take a business class at the local community college?

What about your children? What are their dreams? Are you contributing to them with encouragement? Are you assisting them with taking the practical steps they need to fulfill those dreams?

These are important parts of life that we must model and impart to our children. Holding someone accountable is not supposed to be acting like a brutal taskmaster requiring things from his subjects. It is assisting someone into his or her destiny. There is not a more practical place to learn this than in the home. This must happen first and foremost in our families, where we guard one another's dreams and contribute to each other's destinies.

Families that live this way at home are in a position to bring this Kingdom influence to the rest of their community, most of whom have never been taught this part of life. I am happy that this tool of accountability helps people step into fulfilled dreams. But what really excites me is the thought that it is in community that people really learn how to live life as Jesus intended. Freely.

In some ways, the word *accountability* is one of the best words ever to describe family. Family is to be a unit of people who joyfully work together to the end that each one might fulfill his or her purpose in life. It is a group of individuals who take it upon themselves to hold one another accountable to dream big, and then to serve each other to help see those dreams fulfilled.

Alone in a Crowd

Having friends is not a magic pill that fixes everything. People make horrible compromises all the time because they want friends. The writer of Proverbs 5:14 makes a sobering statement in this regard: "I was almost in utter ruin in the midst of the assembly and congregation." Take notice of the condition of this man—*utter ruin*. Also take notice of his location—*in the midst of the congregation*. You can be alone in a crowd. Attending the right meetings, even small groups, does not guarantee that you will enjoy the fruit of fellowship in your life. The two verses prior to this one, verses 12–13, declare why someone could be in the midst of the solution, but not benefit: "How I have hated instruction! And my heart spurned reproof! I have not listened to the voice of my teachers, nor inclined my ear to my instructors!"

This person nearly in utter ruin hated correction and instruction. If ever there were two traits that could enable us to be successful parents, they would be our ability to admit that we don't know it all, seen in the humble expression of our hunger to learn more. And these only work to the degree that I am willing to receive the correction I need to get it right.

Community gives us the context for growth. My hunger to learn and my willingness to be corrected make it work. This is the nature of family, whether we are talking about your home or mine, or the family of God. This is how we mature and have impact. And this is how our children mature on the path to becoming giant-killers.

16

Exposure to the Supernatural

OUR CHILDREN ARE EXPOSED to so many horrible things by the time they reach adulthood. From the perverted media, to a school system without moral boundaries, to peer pressure that they face in almost every social setting, the exposure is there. I wish I knew the formula for preventing this evil. I don't. But setting values and our intentional parenting can go a long way in providing protection where possible, and understanding, wisdom and discernment where we are unable to keep our kids from negative exposures. Pray for wisdom. And pray often.

Having said that, I know it is possible once again to choose the positive things my family should be exposed to. We have just looked at exposing our children to world need and to community, both of which are vital. The bottom line is, however, that I want my family exposed to God. He is the God of power, purity and love. And I want my children to encounter this wonderful Father who knows us all so well and is completely committed to us as His children. I want them exposed to the Bible as God's Word. Plus, I want them exposed to the God of the Bible, who is the same today, yesterday and forever. He must be relevant and now. He is the Great I AM.

I guess it is a given for us to want our children to encounter God. I have fought specifically for my children to see and experience an authentic move of God through the years. If God was doing it, I wanted it for myself and for my family. I traveled when necessary and spent time with heroes of the faith whenever possible. It was a fundamental responsibility of mine to make sure that my household was exposed to the *more of God*.

We all have different kinds of opportunities in front of us. Some of them are major chances for significant change. Others are more subtle. If we take the ones God has given us, He will give us more, and the opportunities will grow in significance. You attract what you hunger for.

The Distinguishing Mark

There is a very interesting verse, Joshua 24:31, that is repeated almost word for word in Judges 2:7. In the book of Joshua it reads, "Israel served the LORD all the days of Joshua and all the days of the elders who survived Joshua, and had known all the deeds of the LORD which He had done for Israel." Joshua was a spiritual father to a nation. I want to use his example here to illustrate our need for this kind of exposure to the supernatural deeds of God.

The point that this twice-repeated passage makes is that what distinguished Joshua and his leadership team was his exposure to the works of God. When new leaders who had not been exposed to the supernatural interventions of God came up into their positions of rule, they were less likely to inspire a nation to serve God wholeheartedly. But why?

Why would the following generation of leaders not be as successful in their impact on a nation? It was Joshua's exposure to the supernatural activities of God that affected his capabilities and leadership skills. Something was changed on the inside of this great leader by his exposure. The effect of this discovery is far-reaching. The application of this concept to parenting is inspiring!

188

We should all dream of inspiring people to love God with all their heart. Joshua did that for a whole nation. They were successful because his impact was genuine and significant. We live for such impact.

God inspired the writing of Scripture, where it is recorded that Israel followed God as long as Joshua or his elders were still alive. And the only thing mentioned that would distinguish them as different from any other well-intentioned leader in Israel's history was the fact that they were exposed to the supernatural deeds of God.

I cannot imagine how Joshua would have received greater leadership skills merely by seeing manna on the ground every day. Or how water coming out of a rock would give him better insights for his responsibility to lead a nation. I don't think this passage in Scripture is about his abilities, but it could be said that exposure to the supernatural had an effect on him in ways that will never show up on a leadership skills chart. Joshua obtained an acute awareness of God with him, and of the unseen possibility in any situation. It changed his perspective on reality, along with his consciousness of the invisible realm, where he had no control and little understanding. Yet he trusted the God of all things. It was this reality that turned Joshua into a leader people would follow with joy. He was able to draw from a different resource, simply because of what he had seen.

God's kind of leaders lead best when they live conscious of the following facts:

1. Nothing is impossible.
2. God is very personal and is aware of our thoughts and intents.
3. We are not God.
4. God is not under our control.
5. All of us will give an account to God for our lives.

An awareness of these basic realities contributes to living the supernatural lifestyle that Joshua modeled for us.

The Effect of the Miraculous

Joshua was there when the water came out of the rock. He was there to see both the Red Sea and the Jordan River part so that Israel could walk out of bondage, into freedom. He saw the fire of God's presence by night and the cloud of God's presence during the day. Joshua's exposure to the supernatural aspects of God's nature was historic.

Above all that, Joshua had an unusual appetite for God Himself, as seen in the way he would stay at the tent of meeting after Moses would go out from it to speak to the people: "Thus the Lord used to speak to Moses face to face, just as a man speaks to his friend. When Moses returned to the camp, his servant Joshua, the son of Nun, a young man, would not depart from the tent" (Exodus 33:11). There is no doubt that Joshua encountered the God of glory in ways that cannot be expressed. He loved the presence of God.

Whereas Joshua was the leader of a nation, you are the leader in your home. And the principle of *the effect of being exposed to the supernatural* is still real for us. What greater thing could you give to your children than for you to be someone who has been exposed to the supernatural interventions of God?

If I can take this a step further, while it is important for me to see the works of God for myself and influence my children as a result, it is exponentially more powerful to have my children see them as well. This is a priority for us as parents that will cost time, money and great risk. It must, as it will leave a permanent mark of God on our children.

Our Friends the Prophets

Beni and I worked hard to take the spookiness out of the supernatural, but I did not want to make the supernatural so common that it could be disregarded. So you understand there is kind of that strange tension—you don't want to make the supernatural so aloof and so distant that nobody can approach it, but you also don't want to make it so casual that it is disrespected.

The prophetic was a very important part of our life. Several times a year, we had guests come to the church to minister in Weaverville. They ministered in power, having great influence over our church family. And some of them were prophets. Our joy was to host them in our home for meals and times of fellowship.

When there are genuine prophets in the house, the kind of ministers who love God and His people, they serve with such power and wisdom. We fed off these special times with them for many years. God used these times to shape who we were through these wonderful servants of God.

There are two men in particular who served us the most: Dick Joyce and Dick Mills. Interestingly, Dick Mills mentored Dick Joyce for a season in his early years in the charismatic movement. These men had an unusual gift of speaking the precise word of the Lord for the moment to whomever they talked to. It was beautiful to watch and learn from.

God used these men to bring powerful words of encouragement and insight to our church for years. It was fun in a small town to see people receive personal words from God, because we knew most everyone in the room. In one particular meeting, Dick Mills asked me to pick out half a dozen people or so for him to minister to. I went about picking those who stood out to me, including one couple who had almost lost their baby to crib death. They found the child blue and not breathing. Thankfully, a medical team was able to manage a resuscitation. These parents were terrified that it might happen again. When I brought them before Dick, I said nothing about their situation to him. In fact, I never said anything to him about any of the people he was about to minister to, or about the circumstances they were facing.

When Dick grabbed this couple's hands, he smiled really big and declared, "Your home is the safest home in America!" He then followed by giving this couple many promises in the Bible about the safety God had promised to them.

Hope was tangible that day. Everyone witnessed God's very personal touch on a family we loved and cared for. The references to any

Scriptures quoted during such ministry were always written down for the recipients so they could feed their hearts on what God said. It was so beautiful. So personal. They never had another problem with their child. Their home indeed was safe.

Dick Mills had over seven thousand promises of the Bible memorized in multiple translations. From that vast reservoir, God would show him what fit a given situation. Through this kind of ministry, God was so merciful to restore confidence in the prophetic to a part of the Body of Christ who had rejected it because of past abuse. Many Christians who had been turned off to the prophetic were deeply affected by Dick's words to them. It is hard to argue with the use of Scripture.

Both Dick Mills and Dick Joyce ministered to my family and me on many occasions. They would see the treasure planted deeply in one of my kids, and they would call it out. They were always so generous with their time and affection. I am forever indebted to them for the deposit they made into my home.

Not a Perfect Schedule

What you value will be seen in how you manage your time. If I say that my wife is the most important person to me, but I don't take any time for her, you have reason to question my statement. Schedules and checkbooks reveal much about our priorities.

Whenever we live in a place where inconvenience is normal, we live in a place of sacrifice. And fire (God) always falls on sacrifice.

The schedule of these special midweek events with our prophet friends was seldom family friendly. This means it was always a hassle to get the family fed and to the meeting, and then to get the kids to bed at a somewhat reasonable hour. Yet attending this kind of an event was nonnegotiable for my household and me. It seemed too likely that God might show up and do something life changing for all in the room, and I did not want anyone in my family to miss it. So we were there. Always. No exceptions. Even as I write this, I can hear the well-thought-out objections. I knew them then, as I do now. I did not care. We were all in.

You might correctly say that I had to attend these events as the pastor. And that would be true, but only in part. This is the way I live even when my job does not require it. I am involved in countless events every year where I am not required to be there. But I am there. I need more. So much more. And while God knows my address, that He might bring me what I need, I also know His. He is among the saints: "You also are being built *together* into a *dwelling of God* in the Spirit" (Ephesians 2:22, emphasis added). There are some things in God you will only find in the corporate gathering.

My value for the corporate meeting is extremely high, even when it seems that little is happening. Jesus appeared to 500 people after His resurrection (see 1 Corinthians 15:6). But there were only 120 in the Upper Room on the Day of Pentecost, when the Holy Spirit was poured out. Was it because the 500 were not told to come together and pray? Did they have something else to do? Was the ten-day prayer meeting too much for 380 of them? I really don't know. But I do know that I ache for my children and grandchildren to see more than I have seen, to experience more than I have experienced and to be launched in life far beyond what I will ever become or accomplish. To do so, they must have their own divine encounter. And that rarely happens in the casual settings of the average household or church.

Lifelong Indebtedness

I owe my children more than family devotions. I owe them more than being a good example of what it is to be a Christian. I owe them an encounter with the God of all might and power, because that is what changes people for the long haul.

One of the statements I make to our church family is, *Most of what you need in life will be brought to you. But most of what you want, you'll have to go get.* God is so generous and kind that you can live life in the position of receiving all the time and probably do it well. My concern is that we often settle for what is brought to us conveniently. Yet we were born for more, and we know that deep in our hearts.

There are some things we must obtain in the fight, in the pursuit and in the trenches. They will not come to us. I must cry out and go after these things in faith. This is my posture, especially for my children and grandchildren. This is the tension between resting and fighting, between receiving and apprehending and between living as a child of God and living as a responsible soldier of Christ. It is both/and.

It may be impossible to be involved in everything. This is especially true at a place like Bethel. One of our elders jokingly said, "We should change our name to *Denny's—Always Open.*" The schedules are too unreasonably full for any one person to attend everything. That is not the point. Just do something out of the ordinary, something that will cost time and effort. Pray for direction so your time will be spent well and so your children will encounter Jesus. Remember, just one touch changes everything.

Our Own Move of God

I attended a conference at the Vineyard in Anaheim, California, in the spring of 1987, that became a personal turning point. I was so hungry for God to do more in my life. While I cannot say I experienced anything unusual, people started getting healed upon my return home. This had *never* happened before. The God of power seemed to enter the room, and things started happening that I had read about but had never seen personally.

I remember one meeting where I ministered to all our children at church. The Holy Spirit began to touch these children so powerfully. I will never forget it. Eric, around twelve at the time, was ministering with me. He started to pray for one particular child and then felt the Holy Spirit telling him to wait a moment and He would show him whom to pray for. He then prayed for a different child, who was powerfully touched by God. Later that night, the parent called our home to ask what had happened. This might sound a little strange, but that child could not talk for several hours and would weep whenever anyone mentioned the name of Jesus. God had put His mark on that child, and it became an unusual, but treasured experience.

Children are born for the move of God, and we have to do all we can to expose them to it. I once took Brian to India with me to minister alongside Dick Joyce to a crowd of many thousands of hungry people. The people loved Brian and kept touching his blond hair. Exposure, exposure, experience, experience. This must be our mandate for our children. While we cannot force them to experience anything, we can make them hungry and available.

One time, I brought my family to a conference in another city where I was speaking. They swam in the pool and went shopping during the day. But they attended the meetings with me at night. I remember one particular time of praying for people around the altar. It was so powerful, and in the middle of it all Eric came to me, weeping. He asked me to pray for him because he had not heard God speak to him in about three weeks. I did pray, but I felt as though I should have had him pray for me!

And Yet Again

In 1995, we had another outpouring of the Holy Spirit. It happened in the months following my first visit to Toronto. What was happening there was contagious, and by then most of our church family was being impacted in such a transformational way. It was so beautiful. This time was much more powerful than the previous outpouring. In part, it was because I did not know how to sustain a move of God in 1987. I did not realize that it is God who lights the fire on the altar, but it is the priests who keep it burning. A fire will never die out if it has fuel to burn. We become the fuel for the fire. Yielded hearts burn well.

This 1995 outpouring affected everything in our lives. Everything. Miracles, transformed lives, unusual experiences in our meetings—all of this became the norm in this new season. It was this season that God used to shape so many things about our family. We truly were born for the moves of God.

Then, a few years ago, when we started having unusual manifestations of what looked like gold dust in a cloud and things of that nature in our services, I did not know what to do—whether I should hit the ground, or hide or worship. A manifestation would just come, unexpectedly. And then I started watching the children. They would run with their mouths and arms wide open. With no hesitation, they would run into the middle of it, as if to say, "God is here, and I'm going to enjoy Him!" And I thought to myself, *Maybe I should follow them.*

The point is, the kids were there. It is vital for us to choose our moments well so that our children stay exposed—not just to video testimonies, as much as I love those—but to seeing something happen, seeing somebody touched and filled with joy, seeing somebody weeping and coming to Christ, seeing somebody confessing sin, seeing somebody being delivered from the torment he or she has suffered. It is important for our kids to see God at work, not just see people doing God's work.

Wise Men Still Travel

I remember sensing a grace on our son Eric for evangelism, so I took him out of town to hear Mario Murillo. Mario was the man God used to turn my heart into an affectionate lover of Jesus. I am forever indebted to him for that and so much more. He is also uniquely gifted for the miraculous. He is often used to bring extreme miracles to the desperate needs of people, for the glory of God. Mario also came to Weaverville to minister. What a treat to be with my friend, the one to whom I owe so much. His impact on our church, and on my personal family, is significant.

Having my family exposed to those who function differently than I do is of extreme importance. And when such people do so in power, we must be there to support, receive and learn. It is vital that my descendants see the impossibilities of life bow to the name of Jesus through the lips of a believer. They must, in turn, learn to speak the same way and see the same results.

It is so much easier when what you long for is happening at your home church, or at least in your hometown. That is obviously not the case for most people. In that situation, you pray for it in your home, pray for it in your church and pray for it in your city. Cry out to God. He will not disappoint! But until you have personal break-through, travel when possible. I often advise people to go with one of my best friends, Randy Clark of Global Awakening Ministries. He takes people all over the world on ministry trips. Most people will see more miracles on one of his trips than many miracle-working ministers would see in several years of service. Literally. But the most fun part is that this grace for healing and miracles is contagious. It will follow you home. If it is ever possible, take your family on such a trip. I cannot imagine a more significant way to impact the destiny of a family than this.

We have many families that travel to Bethel for their vacations. A number of children have chosen a trip to be with us instead of choosing Disneyland or other exciting vacation destinations. Last week I met another young lady who attended for a few days. It was her birthday gift. Honeymooners visit, getting all they can. People are becoming so hungry that they will do whatever is needed to encounter God in a more profound way. And this is what we owe to ourselves and then to our families. Our exposure to the supernatural interventions of God will change us forever. When that is passed on to a generation of growing giant-killers, their impact is profound, lasting a lifetime.

17

Warfare Made Practical

THE HOME IS THE PLACE for acceptance, joy, celebration and work. It is the place where our children learn responsibility, but the reward also becomes more and more apparent. Parents carry the mandate to make their homes havens of peace.

A reality we discussed earlier is that we were born into a war. This is truer than most would like to admit. And while it has been a goal of mine never to live overly devil conscious, it has also been a goal not to be tricked by his devices. He lies, manipulates, accuses, distracts, divides and works to draw us away from our privileged assignment in life. He came to steal, kill and destroy. If I see loss, death and destruction, I know he has been present. But Jesus came to give life. And His life conquers all death, loss and destruction, transfusing eternity into our veins now.

I tried to help each of my children learn about the devil's devices so that they would understand when he is trying to trick them into his way of thinking. So often, the battle is for the mind. To illustrate this, I want to relate a story about my son Brian. This happened in a highly challenging season of his life.

Invasions in the Night

Brian was the one who at a very early age would sense when Beni got up early to pray. Moms of small children would understand this challenge—to find a time and place where there are no little ones who need your undivided attention. Beni would rise, oh so quietly, and go to the living room, near the heat of the woodstove. She has always loved taking quality time to be with Jesus. But Brian somehow knew when she was praying. He would come with his blanket and cuddle next to her without talking or asking for anything. He may have been the first one in our family to "soak" in the presence of the Lord. Beni seemed to have the sense that he was attracted to the moment, as he had an inbuilt hunger for the presence of the Lord.

When Brian was about seven years old, he began to have tormenting things happen to him in the night. He would come to me with the most horrified look in his eyes, as torment would hit him. Now, I know who I am in Christ, and I am well aware of my authority. But this seemed to come to us at a level I was not accustomed to.

I prayed with Brian before he went to bed, making sure he knew who he was in Christ, and who God was to him. But little changed. I remember one night when he came into our room absolutely terrified. I put him in bed next to me, and Beni went into the other room so she could pray, but then also sleep.

As we lay in bed, I began to teach Brian about spiritual warfare. There are four weapons I had become aware of that I wanted him to learn to use. Doing so would enable him to live a lifestyle of victory. Without learning to use these tools, he would have to depend on others for help.

I am sure you have heard the illustration of giving a man a fish versus teaching him to fish. If he is given a fish, he has a meal. If he is taught to fish, he can feed himself for a lifetime. That same concept was at work here. If Brian learned how to use what God had given him, he would have victory, but he would also be able to

200

impart it to others. If he did not learn to use the weapons himself, he would have to depend on the help of others to be okay. The four weapons are these:

1. The blood of Jesus
2. The Word of God
3. The name of Jesus
4. Praise

In the night, he and I would discuss every weapon and how to use it, and then we would practice what I discussed with him. Our conversations went like this:

The blood of Jesus sets us free. It is because of the blood that we have a legal right to every victory in Christ for all eternity. It is through the blood that we have been set aside, away from ordinary use, for the purposes of the King and His Kingdom. Pleading the blood of Jesus over our lives is only to emphasize by faith the reality that already exists for us.

The Word of God is a most powerful weapon. I remember praying over a young man who had been in an accident. His brain waves were gone, as were his vital signs. The doctors were keeping him alive by machines. I came into the emergency room and prayed over him, declaring the Word of the Lord over his life. He woke up the next morning, totally fine. It is by the Word of the Lord that creation was made. And it is by the Word of the Lord that we are equipped to fight. Paul told Timothy to fight according to the prophecies made concerning him (see 1 Timothy 1:18). God still speaks, but never in contradiction to His Word. When He speaks to us, He is equipping us to win the battle over our destinies.

The name of Jesus is the name to which every knee will bow, and every tongue will confess that Jesus Christ is Lord. This is Reality 101. The devil fears the name of Jesus. He does not fear mine. But he fears me as I function in Jesus' name. He truly trembles before anyone who knows the power of that name. Using the name of Jesus is to find refuge in His name. It is a tower of strength, a hiding place in battle (see Proverbs 18:10). Learning this tool is vital for every believer.

Praise is so powerful. David seems to be the one who discovered this truth. When God is lifted high in praise, His enemies are scattered (see Psalm 68:1–2). There is so much information on this subject in Scripture that you almost have to read His Word with blinders to miss it. Praise is a weapon that is so effective that it becomes tempting to give God praise just to win a spiritual conflict, instead of making it the tool we use to bring Him glory. He is the One who makes praise powerful against the powers of darkness. Isaiah 42:10–13 illustrates this well. Praise is God focused, not devil focused. That distinction will help us in learning to use these weapons effectively.

New Converts

I remember a couple that had just given their lives to Christ. They were a bit panicked because when they would pray, their child would start growling in an obviously demonic manifestation. Sometimes, parents' lifestyles before receiving Jesus give their children a number of opportunities to become demonized.

I gave this dad a brief lesson on warfare and told him to pray over his sleeping child at night. He did so, and that first night the child flopped around on the bed, but then became peaceful. Deliverance came, and their child woke up normal and free the next morning!

Parents always have this kind of authority. Yet in our fight for Brian, I had to use his will and obedience as part of our victory. Little did I understand then what I know now—that God uses the devil's strategy against him by making the targeted area of weakness into a new area of strength. This is all by the grace of God. And Brian's life is now a testimony to this fact.

The Battleground Called Night

As always, I would pray with Brian before he went to bed, as I did with all three of my children. I would pray specifically concerning this issue of night terrors. After he was in bed sleeping, I would go in again to pray over him some more. Yet he would often wake up dealing with the same issue.

He would then come into my room again, while Beni would go into the spare room to sleep. I never minded in the least. We needed to win this one together. We would talk about a biblical principle of victory, and then pray and worship. Praise became a primary weapon for Brian, as it has been for me. Sometimes we would declare the Word of God until breakthrough came. Brian would eventually come into a place of peace again and drift off to sleep.

I remember one night in particular when I told him to come into my room anytime he needed me, but that I wanted him to try something first. "Before you come to get me," I said, "see if God will give you a word to use for your own victory."

He never came in that night. When we sat down for breakfast, I excitedly asked him if all was well, because he had never come into my room. He said it was a horrible night. So I asked him why he had not come to get me. He said it was because he had done what I said. He had asked God to speak to him from His Word. God was so generous in giving him exactly what he needed, and he can quote that Scripture to this day. It became part of his arsenal of weapons to use against the wiles of the devil.

Sometimes our victories come in a moment, often preceded by a very specific action that God directed. But other times, our victory comes rather slowly and is connected to our growth. The latter would be the case for Brian. While there were moments of breakthrough, the overall issue diminished as he grew into the man God had created him to be. As usual, the devil overplayed his hand. Today Brian exercises great authority over this issue, helping countless numbers of people with similar problems. His personal victory became a corporate blessing. He has now led countless people into freedom. His life now shouts *Liberty through Jesus!*

The Table of the Lord

I already mentioned the blood of Jesus as a weapon, but I would like to focus more clearly on this part of our lives as it is found in the Eucharist—Communion. This is one of the more special moments in the life of the believer. This is where we honor the Lord by remembering His death and resurrection, and we proclaim His soon-coming return.

Beni and I like to take Communion every day. In reality, that means we partake of this momentous meal very often. Sometimes we do so together, sometimes individually. Regardless of when or how often we partake, this has become a primary tool of our lives for the sake of our family.

In an earlier chapter, I presented the story of how Job would offer sacrifices for his children after they had a birthday celebration or shared in other big events together (see Job 1:4–5). This was his intercessory role, which the Bible says he did continually. I love this! Job's example has always stirred my heart for my children. He did not wait for them to sin, and then cry out to God on their behalf. He cried out to God just in case they might have become careless in their hearts. He did this during their time of blessing, not only in crises. This is so stunning to me. In light of that principle, I want to discuss Communion—the broken body and the shed blood of Jesus. Beni has a wonderful new book on this subject, *The Power of Communion.**

The Bread

The bread is the broken body of Jesus. He became broken, that we might become whole. He became empty, that we could be full. He

---

*See Beni Johnson, *The Power of Communion: Accessing Miracles through the Body & Blood of Jesus* (Destiny Image, 2019).

became rejected, that we could be accepted. He became sin, that we could become righteous. The list goes on and on. He bore our brokenness, our affliction, our disease and our torment all upon Himself so we would not have to do so for ourselves.

The broken body is His torn flesh. His flesh was torn during His beating, when He was whipped. Concerning these tears in His flesh, Scripture says by His stripes you were healed (see 1 Peter 2:24). When I hold the bread out before the Lord, I make confession of what God has said. It goes something like this: "By the stripes of Jesus, I was healed." I then move on to praying for friends who are suffering with physical issues: "By the stripes of Jesus, Mary was healed. Cancer, be gone!"

I continue with that form of praying with declaration until I am finished with those people He brings to mind. One of Beni's friends had multiple terminal diseases, and Beni encouraged her to take Communion every day. She did. Within a couple of months, she was healed of them all. This is what Jesus suffered for as He died.

The Blood

It is the blood of Jesus that sets us free. It was the shedding of the innocent blood of the Lamb of God that rendered both the record and power of sin forever defeated in the life of the believer.

When I hold the cup before the Lord, I like to make confession and proclamation again. I declare with authority, "As for me and my house, we will serve the LORD" (Joshua 24:15). I remind the Lord of the fact that in the Old Testament, one lamb was sacrificed per household. And that was through an inferior covenant. I want every one of my descendants to serve Him wholeheartedly and with great joy. And so I pray to that end.

I then mention every family member by name, according to each household—Eric and Candace, with their daughters, Kennedy and Selah; Brian and Jenn, with their children, Haley, Téa, Braden and Moses; Gabe and Leah, with their children, Judah, Diego, Isabella and Cruz. I then pray for the blood of Jesus to cover each family member and that God would give each of them a heart to know Him. I also ask God to teach them His ways and that they would know the ways of the Holy Spirit in revival all their days. This is my cry.

From there I move on to other situations in prayer, dealing specifically for the three well-known men who have made it a point to expose me as a heretic or someone outside the faith. Scripture is clear: We are not allowed to criticize the servant of another (see Romans 14:4). These men do not work for me. They work for God. And if God does not defend me, I am not worth defending. In this moment of praying for these leaders in the Body of Christ, I ask God to give them great blessing, such as seeing every child and grandchild serve the Lord with great zeal and joy. I ask God to prosper them in every possible way, that they would never lack in anything.

I move on from these areas of prayer, bringing before the Lord the members of my staff, as well as many close friends. But my point should be clear: The time of Communion is a very special time for me before the Lord, to give Him honor and praise for His priceless work, as well as to join in intercessory prayer on behalf of my family.

I remember several years ago hearing of a woman who prayed like this for her extremely rebellious son. As she held the cup before the Lord, she acknowledged that the blood of Jesus was enough for her son and that she was claiming his soul. Within a few hours, he called in full repentance.

Please Try This at Home

As I understand life in this Kingdom, the power of God/will of God is released through us in three specific ways: a decree, the act of faith and a prophetic act. Let's look more closely at these.

Decree—This is where we say what God is saying. Jesus never prayed for the sick that we can find. But He would speak to an issue, whether it be a demon, a disease or condition, or the environment, like a storm. Sometimes things just need to be said. Life and death are in the power of the tongue. Choose life.

Act of faith—This is where real faith causes us to do something unreasonable. It may be to empty my bank account through giving, when I am the one needing a breakthrough. This action is not a trick to get faith. It is instead the expression of faith.

Prophetic act—This is where an action is required of the Lord that has no logical connection to the desired outcome. The biblical story of the prophet throwing a stick into the water to recover a lost axe head comes to mind (see 2 Kings 6:1–7). You can throw sticks in the water all day long and not get them to make iron swim—unless, of course, God says to throw in a stick.

Each of these three actions is to become a tool that helps bring about breakthrough. Interestingly, both Eric and Brian had very large plantar warts on the bottom of their feet at the same time. The warts were about the size of a dime. We taught the boys to "speak to the mountain," commanding it to be removed in Jesus' name. They did this whenever they thought of it, for many days. One night as we were putting them to bed, we noticed that the wart was completely gone for one of them. When we checked the other, the wart actually fell off in his hand. Some years later, the same thing happened to Leah. She applied the same principle, and the wart disappeared.

A wart is not a mountain. But it does provide good practice for us to learn to demonstrate our purpose and assignment of releasing God's will in the earth. Grab your moments to teach your children about their authority in this wonderful Kingdom.

From the Cross

Jesus did not suffer the way He did so we could attend church. I am not putting church attendance down. I love it. But there is so much more. He purchased us, bringing us into His family, that we might manifest who He is and what He is like to the world. We have the honor to *re*-present Jesus!

In the same way that resurrection followed the cross, so breakthroughs of promise follow our sacrificial parenting. Because He gave Himself to us in the most extreme way possible, so must we live with the awareness that there is nothing He will not do to enable our success in the assignment He has given us. Parenting is a sacred role, patterned after the Father and the Son. We are privileged to embrace this mission with joy, knowing that He is more than sufficient to make up for our weakness and ignorance, ensuring that His victory from the grave would be our victory in the home.

God has chosen our families to have an impact on the course of world history. We have been given all the tools we need to bring about the transformation and discipleship of nations that He longs for. Everything we will ever need was provided for us in the sacrifice of the Lamb of God on our behalf. And it is from the place of His accomplishment that we have the confidence to live, serve and envision the future. For this reason, we have unfailing hope.

This is what Jesus paid for. He longs for us to have children, who have children, who have children . . . who will impact the world with His love, power, wisdom and purity. And it is to this end that we embrace the privilege of *intentional parenting*—raising giant-killers!

10 Things I Wanted
My Children to Know

THIS IS A LETTER I WROTE to my son Eric in June 1994. In it I address the 10 things I wanted my children to know before they left home. While only Eric is mentioned, this letter represents my commitment and focus toward Brian and Leah as well. These were my goals for *intentional parenting.*

My son Eric,

I don't think that it is possible for any dad to love his children more than I love you, Brian and Leah. Each one of you makes me so proud.

The past several months have been difficult for me, all because of tonight's graduation. I have taken much time to think about my role as a father, wondering about my responsibility/ privilege in teaching you the things that matter. Before you were born, I determined to follow God in this assignment. The 18 years have gone by too fast, and I find myself torn—happy for your growth and maturity, but sad that my role is changing. I was just getting started.

In this time of reflection, I have felt somewhat as I did before school finals: nervous, and hoping that I did my part. You have certainly done yours. At any rate, I made a list of important things to learn, very similar to one I made in my heart almost 18 years ago. I'll call them the 10 things that I want my children to learn before they leave home. I have tried to set an example for you in these things. Where I have been weak, He remains strong, and will teach you personally.

1. Learn how to pray, simply.

You know that I've not kept my sins and shortcomings from you. I've wanted you to know my imperfections, and God's commitment to forgive and use anyone willing to serve. When we've had a need, Mom and I have not kept it from you. We didn't want to protect you from being exposed to crises. We wanted you to learn prayer the right way—in the trenches, not just in the classroom.

Prayer can grow by discipline. You can learn from books and from other people's examples. But, in all of your learning, keep it simple. Require of yourself the romance of knowing God, and prayer will never be reduced to duty.

2. You will stand before God and give an account of your life.

I can't imagine a more awesome moment in time than on the day we stand before God to give an account of our life. The Judgment Throne that we will be privileged to stand before as Christians is not one where heaven or hell is the issue. That has forever been settled because of Jesus. The only question that remains is, What did I do with what God gave me? He has given us so much: time, abilities, friends, a heritage, insight, purpose, a call/assignment, and more than could ever be listed in this letter. Please remember, this is the one moment that will matter to you more than all others combined. Invest in it well, for that is when we will hear, "Well done, good and faithful servant."

3. *You are responsible for your own choices.*

I'm sure you remember the many times we worked to drive this point home. You'd come to Mom and me, all upset because of what so-and-so did. You would go on to say, "He makes me so mad." And we would say, "He didn't make you mad; that was your choice." And then there were the times that friends would do something wrong, and you would say that they made you do it with them. And again, our response would be, "It was your choice. Nobody made you." It was hard at first, but you seemed to pick up on that all-important lesson.

In the time that we live in, it is more and more difficult to find people who will not blame others for what oftentimes is the simple result of their own choices. It has become fashionable to blame everyone from teachers, to parents, to society, and even God for whatever calamity comes our way. All of this is the result of people who prioritize their rights over their responsibilities. It's a simple lie with long-lasting devastation. Resist it on all fronts!

You'll get out of life what you put into it, whether it be in ministry, marriage, family, work, recreation, etc. God said it this way: You reap what you sow.

4. *What money is really worth.*

I've learned so much through the years on this subject, and yet I've so much more to learn. These are the most important: Give to God the first and the best; debt grows like weeds, while savings grow like a garden (meaning that, through hard work, you can grow in savings, but doing nothing makes room for debt); generosity and contentment are the two key words for financial success; and don't work to give money to God. Work to honor God with your work, and then honor Him with the fruit of your work.

I had hoped to teach you so much more than I have been able to do. It's because I have been such a slow learner and have not passed all the courses.

211

5. Relationships are worth the high price.

Do you remember how every year, the soccer season and the Little League season would overlap? It seems that there were always about two or three games left on your soccer schedule when your baseball team would begin to practice. It was always such a temptation to skip the soccer and move on to new things. We always required you to finish what you started. Or, as we put it then, "Wherever you made your first commitment is where you are to stay until it's finished." Commitment (or covenant, as the Bible calls it) is the backbone of relationships. Out of that come loyalty and faithfulness. Good relationships have value beyond our ability to comprehend. You will have true biblical wealth if you have just a few lifelong friends. But to have one, you must be one.

One more thing—choose to believe the best about people. Give them the benefit of the doubt. It saves us from a lot of anguish and heartache.

6. Taking care of number one!

We've not protected you from the embarrassing tragedies in the Church—the moral failures of a great number of leaders in the Body of Christ. So many of these men and women fell simply because they tried for so long to give to people more than they had received from God. Such a lifestyle bankrupts us physically, emotionally, mentally and spiritually. From that place of need can come carelessness. And the rest is history. The only antidote is to keep our own storehouses full, meaning, put your own relationship with God first.

When you get on an airplane, the stewardess tells all passengers about how the oxygen mask will come out of the ceiling if it's needed. They always remind the parents, "Put the mask on yourself first, and then put it on your children." To put your relationship with God first is not selfish, any more than it is for the trees outside to reach for the waters of the subterranean streams in the earth. It's what they were made to do. Anything else would not be unselfish; it would be foolish! Putting the mask on yourself first is the guarantee that you'll be around to help others.

7. Be excellent!

If it's worth your time and effort, it's worth doing well. And if you're going to do it well, sacrifice until it is excellent.

We noticed that as a child, you were a perfectionist. Everything had to be just right, to be right. This kind of drive afflicts the careless and convicts the carefree. Yet it is what put the astronauts on the moon, gave Joe Montana four Super Bowl rings and helped two young men develop a new approach to computers from their garage, all the while standing in the shadow of Goliath (IBM), and eventually turning their efforts into the largest computer company in the world. (Yay, Mac!)

You've done this so often in your life. Just don't forget the two biblical guidelines: Whatever your hands find to do, do it with all of your might; and do it as unto the Lord. These two qualifications take our efforts out of the temporal into the realm of the eternal, where they really count.

8. Read the Bible for all it's worth!

I'll never forget the day we bought the International Children's Bible *version for you and Brian. You were about 7 years old. Being the only translation in the world for children (at a third-grade reading level), we hoped you'd understand it more. Standing in the bookstore, I had you read Galatians 2:20, where Paul makes that classic statement, "I do not live anymore—it is Christ living in me." At the conclusion of that verse your eyes lit up, and you said with excitement, "Hey, I understand that!" That Bible could have cost a thousand dollars and I would have found a way to buy one for you. Son, please don't underestimate the power of that book. Armies have marched against it, kings have worked to destroy it and philosophers have prophesied its demise. Yet the Word of God stands as a testimony of God bringing salvation to man. And no power of hell can stop that ongoing testimony.*

In light of that, come to Him often, hungry, humble, broken and in great need. Don't come so that you can teach others. Only teach them what you learn. Make learning your priority. Every answer for every need is available to you in that book, the Bible.

9. Giving faith away.

Once while I was ministering in Spain, I called home to see how you all were doing.

When you got on the phone, you asked if anyone had been saved. I had to explain to you that I was there to work with pastors and Bible school students, and therefore no one had received Christ. That night, I spoke in a church, and a young woman was born again. It's the only time that this has happened on that kind of trip. I believe it was in honor of your concern.

By gifting, you are an evangelist. We've all known that for years. I have been excited because your future is one that will count for eternity.

Do you remember when I used to drive you to Redding to attend a Mario Murillo meeting, encouraging you to "watch the evangelist, because someday you might be in his shoes"?

If you'll make God's heart the focus of your heart, and re-member the value of human life, you'll never lack opportunities to minister this great Gospel to a dying world. And you'll do it with resurrection power!

10. Know what God thinks about you.

His forgiveness is greater than your ability to sin. His plan for you is perfect. It's the only plan that can possibly fully satisfy your heart. He thinks about you all the time. In fact, both Jesus and the Holy Spirit pray to the Father on your behalf 24 hours a day! God sees past your problems and is excited over your potential. He's so confident of your doing well in your life that He is right now preparing a place for you in eternity as part of your reward. He felt you were worth dying for, so that you would find Him worth living for. He never starts the day in a bad mood. His mercies are new every morning! His thoughts for you are great, and worth discovering for yourself.

With Much Love!
Dad

Appendix 2

Home Sunday School Parent's Guide

THIS IS THE PATTERN we adopted thirty-plus years ago in our church in Weaverville. I mention it now as a reference for the kinds of things we can do to assist our kids in learning. In our Sunday school program, each lesson follows a four-part template, while leaving room for personal family "flavoring." The late Larry Richards, whom we greatly admired, created this foundation. He was an author, an educator and the editor of the well-known and widely used *Adventure Bible* and *Teen Study Bible*.

1. **Sharing Love**—Every lesson begins with an activity, with the intent of establishing a relaxed and encouraging atmosphere. Our Sunday school is already within the family setting, so familiarity is not a problem. This initial time, though, is used to set the stage for warm, open communication through either (a) affirming one another with encouraging words, initiated by the parents, or (b) opening up with a suggested question used to stimulate curiosity and conversation about the day's subject matter.

2. **Understanding God's Truth**—This teaching time includes creative learning activities to reinforce each lesson. We remember

217

10 percent of what we hear, 50 percent of what we hear and see and 90 percent of what we hear, see and do!

3. **Exploring God's Word**—This is an opportunity for the truth to be seen in the Scriptures. It is good for the older children to find and read the text themselves, but the younger children enjoy the Bible read to them as a story.

4. **Responding to God's Truth**—Finally, we apply the truth that has been taught. This application time includes acknowledging personal responsibility or suggesting activities to establish the entire family in walking out the truth. Remember, our goal is not just the transmitting of Bible facts; it is to impart "likeness" (see Luke 6:40). Because of that, we must constantly remember to personalize truth and not deal with it abstractly.

Four Cornerstones of Thought— A Declaration

W E OCCASIONALLY READ this confession before receiving an offering. It is one of four offering readings we use at Bethel.* Written by those who serve in our children's ministry, it is based on my teaching on the four cornerstones of thought, which I listed for you in chapter 3. Declared as a confession, it is a practical way to embed these concepts deeply into the heart.

I am powerful.
And what I believe changes the world.
So today I declare,

God is in a good mood.
He loves me all the time.
Nothing can separate me from His love.
Jesus' blood paid for everything.
I will tell nations of what He has done.

*To see all four offering readings, visit https://www.bethel.com/offering-readings/.

I am important.
How He made me is amazing.
I was designed for worship.
My mouth establishes praise to silence the enemy.
Everywhere I go becomes a perfect-health zone.
And with God,

Nothing is impossible!

Appendix 4

Praying the Bible

ERE ARE SOME OF THE VERSES that our family has used in praying for our children and grandchildren, and in my mother's case, her great-grandchildren. This is actually my mother's list, which she gave to all the parents in our family. You will notice that some Scriptures can be prayed and declared "as is." In other cases, the Scriptures present a principle that reveals how or what we need to address in prayer and/or proclamation. I have listed these passages for you in two different translations—the New American Standard Bible (NASB) and the New Living Translation (NLT). I also have often added a third—The Passion Translation (TPT).

Joshua 24:15

NEW AMERICAN STANDARD BIBLE (NASB)
. . . but as for me and my house, we will serve the LORD.

NEW LIVING TRANSLATION (NLT)
But as for me and my family, we will serve the LORD.

Deuteronomy 4:9

NASB

Only give heed to yourself and keep your soul diligently, so that you do not forget the things which your eyes have seen and they do not depart from your heart all the days of your life; but make them known to your sons and your grandsons.

NLT

But watch out! Be careful never to forget what you yourself have seen. Do not let these memories escape from your mind as long as you live! And be sure to pass them on to your children and grand-children.

Psalm 18:50

NASB

He gives great deliverance to His king,
And shows lovingkindness to His anointed,
To David and his descendants forever.

NLT

You give great victories to your king;
    you show unfailing love to your anointed,
    to David and all his descendants forever.

THE PASSION TRANSLATION (TPT)

You have appointed me king and rescued me
    time and time again with your magnificent miracles.
    You've been merciful and kind to me, your anointed one.
    This favor will be forever seen upon your loving servant,
        David,
    and to all my descendants!

Psalm 22:30–31

NASB

Posterity will serve Him;
It will be told of the Lord to the coming generation.
They will come and will declare His righteousness
To a people who will be born, that He has performed it.

NLT

Our children will also serve him.
 Future generations will hear about the wonders of the
 Lord.
His righteous acts will be told to those not yet born.
 They will hear about everything he has done.

TPT

His spiritual seed shall serve him.
 Future generations will hear from us
 about the wonders of the Sovereign Lord.
His generation yet to be born will glorify him.
 And they will all declare, "It is finished!"

Psalm 33:11

NASB

The counsel of the Lord stands forever,
The plans of His heart from generation to generation.

NLT

But the Lord's plans stand firm forever;
 his intentions can never be shaken.

TPT

His destiny-plan for the earth stands sure.
 His forever-plan remains in place and will never fail.

Psalm 37:26

NASB

All day long he is gracious and lends,
And his descendants are a blessing.

NLT

The godly always give generous loans to others,
and their children are a blessing.

TPT

Instead, I've found the godly ones
to be the generous ones who give freely to others.
Their children are blessed and become a blessing.

Psalm 78:1–7

NASB

Listen, O my people, to my instruction;
Incline your ears to the words of my mouth.
I will open my mouth in a parable;
I will utter dark sayings of old,
Which we have heard and known,
And our fathers have told us.
We will not conceal them from their children,
But tell to the generation to come the praises of the LORD,
And His strength and His wondrous works that He has done.

For He established a testimony in Jacob
And appointed a law in Israel,
Which He commanded our fathers
That they should teach them to their children,
That the generation to come might know, even the children
yet to be born,
That they may arise and tell them to their children,
That they should put their confidence in God
And not forget the works of God,
But keep His commandments . . .

NLT

O my people, listen to my instructions.
　　Open your ears to what I am saying,
　　for I will speak to you in a parable.
I will teach you hidden lessons from our past—
　　stories we have heard and known,
　　stories our ancestors handed down to us.
We will not hide these truths from our children;
　　we will tell the next generation
about the glorious deeds of the LORD,
　　about his power and his mighty wonders.
For he issued his laws to Jacob;
　　he gave his instructions to Israel.
He commanded our ancestors
　　to teach them to their children,
so the next generation might know them—
　　even the children not yet born—
　　and they in turn will teach their own children.
So each generation should set its hope anew on God,
　　not forgetting his glorious miracles
　　and obeying his commands.

TPT

Beloved ones, listen to this instruction.
　　Open your heart to the revelation
　　of this mystery that I share with you.
A parable and a proverb are hidden in what I say—
　　an intriguing riddle from the past.
We've heard true stories from our fathers about our rich
　　　　heritage.
　　We will continue to tell our children
　　and not hide from the rising generation
　　the great marvels of our God—
　　　　his miracles and power that have brought us all this
　　　　far.

The story of Israel is a lesson in God's ways.
> He established decrees for Jacob and established the law in
> Israel,
> and he commanded our forefathers to teach them to their
> children.

For perpetuity God's ways will be passed down
> from one generation to the next, even to those not yet born.

In this way, every generation will have a living faith in the
> laws of life
> and will never forget the faithful ways of God.

Psalm 79:13

NASB

> So we Your people and the sheep of Your pasture
> Will give thanks to You forever;
> To all generations we will tell of Your praise.

NLT

> Then we your people, the sheep of your pasture,
> will thank you forever and ever,
> praising your greatness from generation to generation.

TPT

> Then we, your lovers, will forever thank you,
> praising your name from generation to generation!

Psalm 90:16–17

NASB

> Let Your work appear to Your servants
> And Your majesty to their children.
> Let the favor of the Lord our God be upon us;
> And confirm for us the work of our hands;
> Yes, confirm the work of our hands.

NLT

> Let us, your servants, see you work again;
> let our children see your glory.
> And may the Lord our God show us his approval
> and make our efforts successful.
> Yes, make our efforts successful!

TPT

> Let us see your miracles again, and let the rising generation
> see the glorious wonders you're famous for.
> O Lord our God, let your sweet beauty rest upon us
> and give us favor.
> Come work with us, and then our works will endure,
> and give us success in all we do.

Psalm 100:5

NASB

> For the LORD is good;
> His lovingkindness is everlasting
> And His faithfulness to all generations.

NLT

> For the LORD is good.
> His unfailing love continues forever,
> and his faithfulness continues to each generation.

TPT

> For the Lord is always good and ready to receive you.
> He's so loving that it will amaze you—
> so kind that it will astound you!
> And he is famous for his faithfulness toward all.
> Everyone knows our God can be trusted,
> for he keeps his promises to every generation!

Psalm 102:28

NASB

The children of Your servants will continue,
And their descendants will be established before You.

NLT

The children of your people
will live in security.
Their children's children
will thrive in your presence.

TPT

Generation after generation our descendants will live securely,
for you are the one protecting us, keeping us for yourself.

Psalm 103:17–18

NASB

But the lovingkindness of the LORD is from everlasting to
everlasting on those who fear Him,
And His righteousness to children's children,
To those who keep His covenant
And remember His precepts to do them.

NLT

But the love of the LORD remains forever
with those who fear him.
His salvation extends to the children's children
of those who are faithful to his covenant,
of those who obey his commandments!

TPT

But Lord, your endless love stretches
from one eternity to the other,

unbroken and unrelenting toward those who fear you
and those who bow facedown in awe before you.
Your faithfulness to keep every gracious promise you've
made
passes from parents, to children, to grandchildren, and
beyond.
You are faithful to all those who follow your ways
and keep your word.

Psalm 112:2

NASB

His descendants will be mighty on earth;
The generation of the upright will be blessed.

NLT

Their children will be successful everywhere;
an entire generation of godly people will be blessed.

TPT

Their descendants will be prosperous and influential.
Every generation of his godly lovers will experience his
favor.

Psalm 127:3

NASB

Behold, children are a gift of the LORD,
The fruit of the womb is a reward.

NLT

Children are a gift from the LORD;
they are a reward from him.

TPT

Children are God's love-gift; they are heaven's generous reward.

Psalm 128

NASB

How blessed is everyone who fears the LORD,
Who walks in His ways.
When you shall eat of the fruit of your hands,
You will be happy and it will be well with you.
Your wife shall be like a fruitful vine
Within your house,
Your children like olive plants
Around your table.
Behold, for thus shall the man be blessed
Who fears the LORD.

The LORD bless you from Zion,
And may you see the prosperity of Jerusalem all the days of
your life.
Indeed, may you see your children's children.
Peace be upon Israel!

NLT

How joyful are those who fear the LORD—
all who follow his ways!
You will enjoy the fruit of your labor.
How joyful and prosperous you will be!
Your wife will be like a fruitful grapevine,
flourishing within your home.
Your children will be like vigorous young olive trees
as they sit around your table.
That is the LORD's blessing
for those who fear him.

May the LORD continually bless you from Zion.
May you see Jerusalem prosper as long as you live.
May you live to enjoy your grandchildren.
May Israel have peace!

TPT

How joyous are those who love the Lord and bow low before
God,
ready to obey him!
Your reward will be prosperity, happiness, and well-being.
Your wife will bless your heart and home.
Your children will bring you joy as they gather around
your table.
Yes, this is God's generous reward for those who love him.
May the Lord bless you out of his Zion-glory!
May you see the prosperity of Jerusalem
throughout your lifetime.
And may you be surrounded by your grandchildren.
Happiness to you! And happiness to Israel!

Psalm 144:12–15

NASB

Let our sons in their youth be as grown-up plants,
And our daughters as corner pillars fashioned as for a palace;
Let our garners be full, furnishing every kind of produce,
And our flocks bring forth thousands and ten thousands in
our fields;
Let our cattle bear
Without mishap and without loss,
Let there be no outcry in our streets!
How blessed are the people who are so situated;
How blessed are the people whose God is the LORD!

NLT

May our sons flourish in their youth
like well-nurtured plants.
May our daughters be like graceful pillars,
carved to beautify a palace.
May our barns be filled
with crops of every kind.

May the flocks in our fields multiply by the thousands,
>even tens of thousands,
>and may our oxen be loaded down with produce.
May there be no enemy breaking through our walls,
>no going into captivity,
>no cries of alarm in our town squares.
Yes, joyful are those who live like this!
>Joyful indeed are those whose God is the LORD.

TPT

Deliver us! Then our homes will be happy.
>Our sons will grow up as strong, sturdy men
>and our daughters with graceful beauty,
>royally fashioned as for a palace.
Our barns will be filled to the brim,
>overflowing with the fruits of our harvest.
>Our fields will be full of sheep and cattle,
>too many to count,
>and our livestock will not miscarry their young.
>Our enemies will not invade our land,
>and there'll be no breach in our walls.
What bliss we experience when these blessings fall!
>The people who love and serve our God will be happy
>indeed!

Proverbs 11:21–23

NASB

Assuredly, the evil man will not go unpunished,
But the descendants of the righteous will be delivered.
As a ring of gold in a swine's snout
So is a beautiful woman who lacks discretion.
The desire of the righteous is only good,
But the expectation of the wicked is wrath.

NLT

> Evil people will surely be punished,
>> but the children of the godly will go free.

> A beautiful woman who lacks discretion
>> is like a gold ring in a pig's snout.

> The godly can look forward to a reward,
>> while the wicked can expect only judgment.

TPT

> Assault your neighbor and you will certainly be punished,
>> but God will rescue the children of the godly.
> A beautiful woman who abandons good morals
>> is like a fine gold ring dangling from a pig's snout.
> True lovers of God are filled with longings
>> for what is pleasing and good,
>> but the wicked can only expect doom.

Proverbs 14:26

NASB

> In the fear of the LORD there is strong confidence,
> And his children will have refuge.

NLT

> Those who fear the LORD are secure;
>> he will be a refuge for their children.

TPT

> Confidence and strength flood the hearts
>> of the lovers of God who live in awe of him,
>> and their devotion provides their children
>> with a place of shelter and security.

Proverbs 23:24–25

NASB

> The father of the righteous will greatly rejoice,
> And he who sires a wise son will be glad in him.
> Let your father and your mother be glad,
> And let her rejoice who gave birth to you.

NLT

> The father of godly children has cause for joy.
> > What a pleasure to have children who are wise.
> So give your father and mother joy!
> > May she who gave you birth be happy.

TPT

> When a father observes his child living in godliness,
> > he is ecstatic with joy—nothing makes him prouder!
> So may your father's heart burst with joy
> > and your mother's soul be filled with gladness because of
> > you.

Isaiah 38:19–20

NASB

> It is the living who give thanks to You, as I do today;
> A father tells his sons about Your faithfulness.
> The Lord will surely save me;
> So we will play my songs on stringed instruments
> All the days of our life at the house of the Lord.

NLT

> Only the living can praise you as I do today.
> > Each generation tells of your faithfulness to the next.
> Think of it—the Lord is ready to heal me!
> > I will sing his praises with instruments

every day of my life
   in the Temple of the LORD.

Isaiah 44:3

NASB

For I will pour out water on the thirsty land
And streams on the dry ground;
I will pour out My Spirit on your offspring
And My blessing on your descendants . . .

NLT

For I will pour out water to quench your thirst
   and to irrigate your parched fields.
And I will pour out my Spirit on your descendants,
   and my blessing on your children.

Isaiah 49:25

NASB

Even the captives of the mighty man will be taken away,
And the prey of the tyrant will be rescued;
For I will contend with the one who contends with you,
And I will save your sons.

NLT

But the LORD says,
"The captives of warriors will be released,
   and the plunder of tyrants will be retrieved.
For I will fight those who fight you,
   and I will save your children."

Isaiah 51:8

NASB

But My righteousness will be forever,
And My salvation to all generations.

NLT

> But my righteousness will last forever.
>> My salvation will continue from generation to generation.

Isaiah 54:13

NASB

All your sons will be taught of the LORD;
And the well-being of your sons will be great.

NLT

> I will teach all your children,
>> and they will enjoy great peace.

Isaiah 59:21

NASB

"As for Me, this is My covenant with them," says the LORD: "My Spirit which is upon you, and My words which I have put in your mouth shall not depart from your mouth, nor from the mouth of your offspring, nor from the mouth of your offspring's offspring," says the LORD, "from now and forever."

NLT

"And this is my covenant with them," says the LORD. "My Spirit will not leave them, and neither will these words I have given you. They will be on your lips and on the lips of your children and your children's children forever. I, the LORD, have spoken!"

Jeremiah 32:38–40

NASB

They shall be My people, and I will be their God; and I will give them one heart and one way, that they may fear Me always, for their own good and for the good of their children after them. I will make an everlasting covenant with them that I will not turn away from them, to do them good; and I will put the fear of Me in their hearts so that they will not turn away from Me.

NLT

They will be my people, and I will be their God. And I will give them one heart and one purpose: to worship me forever, for their own good and for the good of all their descendants. And I will make an everlasting covenant with them: I will never stop doing good for them. I will put a desire in their hearts to worship me, and they will never leave me.

Luke 1:50

NASB

And His mercy is upon generation after generation
Toward those who fear Him.

NLT

He shows mercy from generation to generation
to all who fear him.

TPT

Mercy kisses all his godly lovers,
from one generation to the next.

Acts 2:17–18

NASB

"And it shall be in the last days," God says,
"That I will pour forth of My Spirit on all mankind;
And your sons and your daughters shall prophesy,
And your young men shall see visions,
And your old men shall dream dreams;
Even on My bondslaves, both men and women,

I will in those days pour forth of My Spirit
And they shall prophesy."

NLT

"In the last days," God says,
  "I will pour out my Spirit upon all people.
Your sons and daughters will prophesy.
  Your young men will see visions,
    and your old men will dream dreams.
In those days I will pour out my Spirit
  even on my servants—men and women alike—
    and they will prophesy."

TPT

This is what I will do in the last days—I will pour out my Spirit on
everybody and cause your sons and daughters to prophesy, and your
young men will see visions, and your old men will experience dreams
from God. The Holy Spirit will come upon all my servants, men and
women alike, and they will prophesy.

Acts 3:25

NASB

It is you who are the sons of the prophets and of the covenant which
God made with your fathers, saying to Abraham, "And in your seed
all the families of the earth shall be blessed."

NLT

You are the children of those prophets, and you are included in the
covenant God promised to your ancestors. For God said to Abraham,
"Through your descendants all the families on earth will be blessed."

TPT

And you are heirs of their prophecies and of the covenants God made
with your fathers when he promised Abraham, "Your descendant will
bring blessing to all the people on the earth."

Acts 16:31

NASB

They said, "Believe in the Lord Jesus, and you will be saved, you and your household."

NLT

They replied, "Believe in the Lord Jesus and you will be saved, along with everyone in your household.

TPT

They answered, "Believe in the Lord Jesus and you will be saved—you and all your family."

Bill and **Beni Johnson** are the senior leaders of Bethel Church in Redding, California. Bill is a fifth-generation pastor with a rich heritage in the Holy Spirit. The present move of God has brought him into a deeper understanding of the phrase "on earth as it is in heaven." Heaven is the model for our life and ministry. Bill and the Bethel Church family have taken on this theme for life and ministry, where healing and miracles are normal. He teaches that we owe the world an encounter with God, and that a gospel without power is not the gospel Jesus preached. Bill is also the co-founder of Bethel School of Supernatural Ministry (BSSM).

Beni is a pastor, author and speaker. She has a call to joyful intercession that is an integral part of Bethel Church. Her insight into strategies for prayer and her involvement in prayer networks bring breakthrough with global impact. She is passionate about health and wholeness—in body, soul and spirit.

Together, Bill and Beni serve a growing number of churches that have partnered for revival. This apostolic network has crossed denominational lines in building relationships that enable church leaders to walk in both purity and power. And as Bill says in these pages, home is the beginning point for having that kind of worldwide impact: "Success at home gives us the authority base to go anywhere else . . . it starts at home."

Bill and Beni's goal at home has always been to raise giant-killers through intentional parenting. Their three children are now married and are all serving with their spouses in full-time ministry. Between them, they have given Bill and Beni ten grandchildren, who are also being raised as giant-killers.